SPECTRUM OF REALITY

Sufi Insights

Spectrum of Reality synthesizes a comprehensive analysis of the human condition and the way we perceive reality. Shaykh Fadhlalla Haeri makes difficult concepts accessible, especially through the use of metaphors, allegories, and insights from modern science.

His thesis is that human consciousness manifests in several ways across a spectrum that ranges from universal supreme consciousness to personal conditioned consciousness. It is the nature of human culture, thought and personal consciousness to continually operate in a dualistic way, so that Reality is obscured by several layers of fragmentation.

The ultimate harmony of human consciousness with universal reality is the challenge of existence. Shaykh Fadhlalla Haeri illustrates that we can heal the split between individual and the universal by recognising that each is essential to its different territory, and believes that 'spirit' is the causal factor from which all states arise.

   Adnan al Adnani, author of Lights of Consciousness: A Sufi view of Science and Spirituality

Reviews on Spectrum of Reality: Sufi Insights

"The aphorisms, precepts and commentaries presented by Shaykh Fadhlallah Haeri in his new work, Spectrum of Reality, are immensely rewarding. They provide the reader an extraordinarly insightful access into the realm of subtle meanings that underpin the outer realities; and provide not only spiritual nourishment but also an understanding of the vaster, hidden, worlds which enfold the human condition."

> Dr. Ali Allawi, visiting professor at the National University of Singapore and Kennedy School of Government, Harvard University, Professor, Oxford University and former Minister of Finance, Iraq, Author of 'The Crisis of Islamic Civilzation', & 'The Occupation of Iraq: Winning the War, Losing the Peace'

"Spectrum of Reality is a true masterpiece, a life long work, and a very well written book, which is sure to satisfy all those who earnestly yearn to know and understand the actual Meaning of Life, What is the Nature of Reality? and How to Awaken to the Divine Self, that is lying latent in each human being, and waiting to be Realised. I highly recommend this significant and priceless publication for all earnest seekers who wish to understand the Real Truth of the World in which we live."

> Alan Jacobs, President Ramana Maharshi Foundation UK, Poet, Author of 'Poetry for the Spirit', 'The Wisdom The Native American Indians', 'When Jesus Lived in India'

Shaykh Fadhlalla Haeri's new work, Spectrum of Reality, is a profound translation. It comes out of the depth of the Sufi tradition of Islam, yet manages to speak without using words that restrict it to that particular tradition. Instead we read about reality, soul, human community, and spirituality. It remains deeply grounded, yet open to all. Recommended for all spiritually seeking readers.

> Dr. Omid Safi, Professor of Asian and Middle Eastern Studies, Duke University & Director of Duke Islamic Studies Center, Author of 'Progressive Muslims: On Justice, Gender, and Pluralism', 'The Politics of Knowledge in Premodern Islam', 'Memories of Muhammad: Why the Prophet Matters'

Shaykh Fadhlalla Haeri offers us a razor-sharp spiritual – yet almost scientific – guide into the nature of reality, and its defining elements: consciousness, connectedness and continuity. Beautifully pedagogically crafted, this book is an invaluable companion on the human quest; profound wisdom emanates from every line and lights the path of the seeker. With the help of Haeri's Spectrum of Reality, one gradually "emerges from the cocoon of identity and separation" and "looks at creation through the lens of oneness". Transcending any religious dogma, this book is a universal gift to humanity and a call to wake up to our true nature. Highly illuminating, highly recommended!

> Prof. Alexander Schieffer, Trans4m Centre for Integral Development, Geneva, Switzerland Co-author of 'Integral Development', 'Integral Economics', 'Integral Research-and-Innovation' and 'Transformation Management'

As an Episcopal priest who is deeply rooted in the truth of her tradition, I need other wisdom teachers to seek what is true in their traditions. There we meet and discover we are One.

Thank you Shaykh Fadhlalla for providing all of us with continued hope and encouragement. I start my morning with your incise invitations to glimpse the truth. Your observations are filled to the brim with liberation and insight. Our cups runneth over. We are blessed.

> The Rev. Jamie L. Hamilton, Rector of All Saints' Church, Peterborough, New Hampshire, USA

This book synthesises a comprehensive analysis of the human condition and the way we perceive reality. It makes difficult concepts accessible, especially through the use of metaphors, allegories, and insights from modern science. Human consciousness is manifested in several ways across a spectrum that ranges from universal supreme consciousness to personal conditioned consciousness. The ultimate harmony of human consciousness with universal reality is the only true arena, but it is the nature of human thought and culture to raise purely conceptual notions of a more limited arena of memory, thought and personal consciousness, continually operates in a dualistic way, so that Reality is obscured by several layers of fragmentation. Shaykh Fadhlalla goes to great lengths to repeat this explanation from several perspectives and his great achievement is to take various ancient and modern views about the nature of reality and to present them alongside his own expanded view.

> Dr. Adnan al Adnani, is a research scientist and inventor with patents in Digital Signal Processing Design for Communications and Test & Measurement. Author of 'Lights of Consciousness'

Human life is a spectrum of experiences. In this book Shaykh Fadhlalla shares his perspectives on the spiritual significance of the spectrum of human experience. In the end he follows the colors of human life back to their Source to remind us of our need to consciously connect to the Light that is eternal.

Shaikh Kabir Helminski, Sufi Master, Poet and author of 'Love's Ripening', 'Rumi and the Journey of the Heart', 'Living Presence', 'The Knowing Heart' and music director for the award-winning, PBS-broadcast documentary 'Muhammad: Legacy of a Prophet'

We thank Shaykh Fadhlalla for this treasure store of deep wisdom, which I am sure I will dip into for many months to come. It appears to encompass everything from the first moment of the big bang to the dimensions of the heart, a journey through all the stages of human and spiritual wisdom, told by someone who has drunk deep from the water where the two seas meet.

Dr. Llewellyn Vaughan-Lee, Lecturer, Author of 'Prayer of the Heart in Christian and Sufi Mysticism', 'Spiritual Ecology: the Cry of the Earth', 'Darkening of the Light: Witnessing the End of an Era'

Shaykh Fadhlalla Haeri's new book Spectrum of Reality sheds light on the mysteries that draw all people towards faith, spirituality, and ultimately, the pursuit of a higher level of consciousness. Like Shaykh Haeri, my experience living both in the Muslim and Western Worlds has taught me that it is essential to understand the similarities among peoples and faiths, rather than focus on our differences. Shaykh Haeri's work substantially contributes to this understanding by illustrating the commonality of our reality, our spirituality, and the divine - beyond political borders and religious differences. In our world of conflict and violence the Shaykh's vision provides a beacon of hope and light.

Professor Akbar S. Ahmed, Ibn Khaldun Chair of Islamic Studies, American University, Fellow at Brookings Institution, Washington DC, USA. Author of 'Journey Into Europe: Islam, Immigration, and Identity', 'The Thistle and the Drone: How America's War on Terror Became a Global War on Tribal Islam', 'Suspended Somewhere Between: A Book of Verse', 'Journey into America: The Challenge of Islam', 'Journey into Islam: The Crisis of Globalization'

SPECTRUM OF REALITY

Sufi Insights

Shaykh Fadhlalla Haeri
Foreword by Neil Douglas-Klotz

Zahra Publications

Publisher: Zahra Publications

ISBN: 978-1-919826-95-0

Typeset by: Quintessence Publishing

Cover design by: Charne Achertberg & Quintessence Publishing

Printed by: Camera Press South Africa

Mandala Images supplied by Gil McIff

Colours changed for printing purposes

www.mandalasacredgeometry.com

http://www.shaykhfadhlallahaeri.com

© 2017 Zahra Publications

All rights reserved. Except for brief quotations in critical articles or reviews, no part of this book may be reproduced in any manner without prior written permission from Zahra Publications.

Acknowledgements

This book was inspired by my lifelong personal quest to experience constant reference and to experience the Ever-Prevailing Oneness in existence. The work went through several levels of manifestations. There were many friends and students who have helped throughout its development. Special thanks to Yunus Ismail, Hashim Ismail, Asia Ndermane, Paul Rischbieter, Zaheer Cassim, Muneera Haeri and Abbas Bilgrami for their heartfelt assistance on this project. Throughout its evolvement, Leyya Kalla nursed this project with patience and loving care. I can only express my gratitude and contentment with the seen and the unseen gifts in creation.

Contents

	FOREWORD by Neil Douglas-Klotz	1
	INTRODUCTION	5
1	**FOUNDATIONS** Setting the scene using basic forces and factors that are often referred to in life.	13
2	**NATURE OF EXISTENCE** Questions of cycles and patterns of entities and forces.	47
3	**CONSCIOUSNESS** Inseparable from life, with many facets and levels.	85
4	**CONNECTEDNESS** The whole universe is interconnected and it is only the intensity and extent that varies.	111
5	**CONTINUITY** Space, time and the speed of light have emerged from a timeless zone and relates to its origin.	135
6	**HUMAN BEINGS** The discernible and physical energy make-up and its relationship to the spiritual life-force within it.	159
7	**PEOPLE** The dynamics of individual and group relationships.	197
8	**TODAY'S WORLD** Emphasis on post-industrial human life and its different facets.	229
9	**SPIRITUALITY** Emphasizing the inner essence of human quests and religions.	267
10	**GUIDANCE** Various important points on the path of awakening for the serious seeker.	307
11	**IT IS** Various items that illustrate diverse aspects of what is real and what is not.	351

SPECTRUM OF REALITY

Foreword

Recent years have seen a number of authors attempt to connect the findings of modern science with mysticism. The discoveries and theories about the way the universe began—on both the microcosmic and macrocosmic levels—have begun to appear more and more like Zen koans. Meanwhile, many people, especially the younger generation, in Western societies have abandoned formal religion. At the same time those who are convinced that their religious path (including scientism) is the "only way" have become more entrenched and threatening towards anyone who does not agree with them. Self-help books abound that seek to reveal a secular spirituality of everyday life. Social networks connect us faster than ever before, but the value of the content conveyed is often as trivial and distracting as it is life-enhancing. Meanwhile, self-harming, depression and obesity are at record levels among Western young people—evidence that the purpose of life seems even more obscure than previously.

In the midst of everything, Shaykh Fadhlalla Haeri has written the most unusual of books. It does not so much connect the findings of modern and post-modern science with mysticism—a conceptual exercise at best—as it shows us how a mystic experiences evolution, black holes, the singularity, cosmogenesis and the quantum reality. Entirely practical, the same gaze illuminates virtually every aspect of everyday life—work, job satisfaction, sexuality, relationships, gender politics, social networks, depression, addiction, corporate greed, consumerism, ecology, political action, and more. Nor does religion and the "God question" escape the same unitive view, but at the same time, the book refuses to use the "special language" of any religious or spiritual tradition. As I said, that most unusual of animals—a book about "life, the universe and everything" without any explicit "God-talk."

The book's title—spectrum of reality—reveals a little more about what we have before us. Each short chapter is only a page long, one colour within the diverse spectrum of life. Like a strong wind blowing away dead leaves, the author's words breathe through and around each topic and settle gently with an aphorism, like a bell rung at the end of a meditation. We find that we are enmeshed in a search for connection and continuity, and that the ephemeral thing we call our "self" arises from a sort of interference pattern within a rainbow of seen and unseen rays, ranging from "how wonderful" to "how terrible." What remains is the real, which Shaykh Fadhlalla—like other mystics—calls the soul.

Yet this is not a book of philosophy or advice. It is not a simplified, powerpoint presentation of spiritual concepts that one can hold onto and feel temporarily satisfied. It is not a grand metaphysical scheme featuring flow charts and hierarchical diagrams. It is not a new age catechism of beliefs that promise to increase one's prosperity, sexual attractiveness or self-esteem. Yet it is perhaps the most practical book that one could read. Everywhere one comes across startling insights that change the way we look at life:

"The mother-child relationship is like putting light to a candle. The baby is like a fresh wick, the mother's gaze sets it alight."

Rather than describe what *Spectrum of Reality* is, perhaps better to describe how one might use it. If you read one chapter each night before retiring or upon arising, the book would accompany you for about a year. When one

FOREWORD

sips rather than gulps, it's easier to breathe. One will find the same insights returning; the important thing is not the insight itself but rather the *way* of experiencing life that Shaykh Fadhlalla breathes into his words. Receive this breath. Or you could close your eyes and breathe a moment in your own heart with an urgent question or challenge that life is presenting now. Then open the book at random. Because the same light connects everything, everywhere and every-when, you will find an answer. If you do this process often enough, you might find that eventually you can manage without having the book around. Open your heart and read the signs of life around you as the wisdom you need. Simple presence within life's spectrum.

Neil Douglas-Klotz (Saadi Shakur Chishti)

Introduction

Life is full of questions and challenges. From childhood onwards we are perpetually seeking answers that may make us feel well and experience harmony, contentment and happiness. A few questions are big and perennial: Who am I? What can I do to experience joy continuously? Who and where is God? How can I access his power, knowledge and eternal state? What is love and how can I be loved? What happens after death? Then there is the classic question: What is consciousness and how does it arise?

The answers to the five questions of Who, What, Where, When and Why are both earthly and heavenly, temporary and perpetual, changing and constant. You are alive because of your soul. You are on this earth in order to complete the experience of inseparability from God and from the source of life and consciousness. The earth is like a divine nursery for human consciousness to stretch from the physical and material to the infinitude of the metaphysical. The completion of evolution is to acknowledge the mind and go beyond it to the original source of life, via the heart.

We deal with dualities all the time and are reconciled when we recognize the unity at origin as well as at final destination. We are middle people caught within space and time, experiencing beginnings and ends, birth and death. We are always in-between. This knowledge can be experienced by transcending the mind and senses. The heart and soul are the means to this realisation.

We seek well-beingness, physical and mental freedom, knowledge, efficiency, the ability to connect, to hear, see and to be able to express ourselves and to be acknowledged. All thoughts and actions are balanced between taking and giving. You inhale and benefit and exhale and benefit. We are hanging on air yet we seek total stability and reliability. This absurd situation contains the seeds of higher wisdom. We always seek meaning and purpose for our thoughts and actions. Our experience of earthly dualities is the foundation of realizing the magic of cosmic unity—ever prevailing.

We experience and enjoy humanity as we awaken to the majesty of divinity. We are balanced between head and heart. We have a physical body, which is subject to countless chemical, physical and other processes. We understand the nature and the psyche of most of creation. We are also driven to discover the source of life and its purpose. We want to have clear and sharp senses, good eyesight and hearing, in addition to evolving inner senses, such as imaginal and reflectiveness. We are on earth as part of the universe; we care for survival, which is an expression of our love for life, knowledge and consciousness. Our body, mind and identity may change but we quest constancy, reliability and security. Life is to do with being sentient and that implies awareness, interaction and the combination of having an identity whilst experiencing countless realities.

INTRODUCTION

We love life, consciousness and appropriate connections and continuity. Illumination is to know that anything to do with the mind and senses is a temporary reality, which symbolizes a greater meaning. What we seek in enlightenment is to witness existence through the lens of Oneness. Life on earth is a beautiful journey for those who are awakened; it becomes a liberating process from all illusions except the Real.

This book explores the mystery of countless dualities that emerge from unity and submerge back into it. It presents sketches and maps illustrating the connections between meanings and forms, the levels and zones of consciousness and human experiences, the direction and purpose of life, and the ultimate destiny of the universe.

The natural human drive is to evolve to a state of consciousness, wholesomeness and understanding with inner contentment at all times; to be balanced and integrated in body, mind, heart and soul. The awakened being accesses joy and goodness at heart without denying pain or pleasure. The higher zone of consciousness is the source of conditioned states of dualities and change. The awakened being experiences existence through the lens and light of the soul and its complete consciousness.

Human nature in its physical, mental and spiritual sense follows a natural evolutionary course driving towards a higher state of consciousness, which is beyond the limitations of space and time. Unhappiness signals deviation from this evolutionary course and the interplay between humanity and divinity and the sacred essence of the soul or the spirit within. The human being is a divine light experiencing countless earthly uncertainties. We witness Reality through the lens of unity.

This book highlights different facets which reflect truth and reality. There is a mysterious and unique light or energy from which the universe had emerged and through which it is sustained and to which it returns. During the past few thousand years, many shamans, prophets, philosophers, seers and sages had emerged, propelled by the power and the force of the discovery of this majestic One Reality.

Human consciousness spans terrestrial and celestial realms. We are cosmic creatures in essence. Even physically, we are made of cosmic dust. Our body, mind and heart draw life from the soul and the spirit. We experience life and consciousness with a beginning and an end and are passionate about a life that does not end. That state belongs to our soul, and is not bound by space or time. We experience limited consciousness and yearn for total or complete consciousness. We experience confused and disturbing consciousness whilst yearning for peace and supreme consciousness.

Three complementary forces fuel all quests and movements in life. These are the passion for life and consciousness, to experience connectedness and continuity or perpetuity of life. The human soul is constrained by space and time whilst on earth, whereas its nature is boundless. We want to shrink distance and space. We love to experience closeness and reduce the feeling of separation. As for continuation, it is the quest for eternity.

INTRODUCTION

That too is the nature of the soul—all of our drives in life are to do with ending distance or time.

Much of this book is an attempt to reveal the true foundation of what appears as real. To peel away transient realities and realize their root is spiritual growth and evolvement. Our culture and civilization reinforces much of the illusions which cause suffering, whereas the soul is utterly content and secure. Brief sketches of higher consciousness and insights are presented, some of which may be the reverse of what is commonly considered true.

This book is an attempt to present a condensed human map of body-mind-self and heart-soul-spirit. Your body is your physical presence including your brain. Mind connects matter with the energy zone. Self is your overall state and condition at any moment. Heart is the metaphoric home of your personal soul, the source of life and consciousness. Spirit denotes the Cosmic Soul and the source of supreme consciousness and life. Your soul is God's light within and spirit is God's cosmic light. Now that you have these navigational aids, you are on your journey to the city that you were aiming for, and the destiny you had hoped for. That city was always embedded within your soul. This truth is not subject to space and time, and as a human, you cannot deny the consciousness of movement, change and growth. Using this atlas of life as a reference for navigation, you will realize the wisdom behind suffering as it prepares you to accept the grace of divine offering. You will be at peace with humanity and your ego as you will be in unison with the sacred spirit and its miraculous gifts.

SPECTRUM OF REALITY

All human hopes and aspirations come to the doorway of a healthy, clear mind and a transparent pure heart. A clear mind brings integrity and wholesomeness to the self, and a pure heart enables the soul's effulgent light to shine and energize all.

Head implies mind, memory, emotion and self. Heart implies soul and spirit which are the source of life. Empathy is when the 'head' is reduced in seeing otherness. Body, mind and self are covered by conditioned consciousness, while heart, soul and spirit relate to higher and complete consciousness. Each of these terms have a certain fluidity as what they represent connects to others, for example, the term self stretches from the animal to the higher self, which connects to heart and soul.

It may appear that some ideas and thoughts have been often repeated. It is more a matter of overlaps and connections rather than repetition. The light of the soul acts as a central point to all experienced realities. The threads of this centre hold together all the numerous thoughts, ideas and concepts in this book. Fairly regularly part of that thread becomes evident, and that too gives the illusion of repetition.

Please meditate upon this work as a whole and avoid reading it only through the lens of reason and rationality – that is only half the story. Approach this book as a lead into deep meditation, rather than for analysis. You are One. Anything that you experience is only an aspect of the same One.

INTRODUCTION

These sketches or maps may allow you to navigate through the intricate visible and invisible realities of life. They may help to bring balance to humanity and divinity through a healthy union between head and heart, mind and soul.

Shaykh Fadhlalla Haeri

I. Foundations

SPECTRUM OF FOUNDATIONS

- ✠ Emergence
- ✠ Dualities & Oneness
- ✠ Self & Soul
- ✠ Form & Meaning
- ✠ Nursery Earth
- ✠ Levels Of Consciousness
- ✠ Attraction & Repulsion
- ✠ Evolution & Natural Selection
- ✠ Space, Time & Infinitude
- ✠ Physics & Metaphysics
- ✠ Matter & Energy
- ✠ Big Bang & Collapse
- ✠ Realities & Reality
- ✠ Directional Randomness
- ✠ Normal & Unusual
- ✠ Religion & Belief
- ✠ Saints & Villains
- ✠ Knowledge & Love
- ✠ Justice & Injustice

SPECTRUM OF REALITY

- Happiness & Misery
- Balance & Rationality
- War & Peace
- Wealth & Poverty
- Quantity & Quality
- Obsession & Passion
- Quest For The Best
- Human Mirroring
- Power Of The Gaze
- Why?

Introduction

Due to consciousness, we perceive a wide range of experiences. Some are important for growth and survival, and others help in our journey towards higher levels of consciousness. The universe's story and biography began with a hydrogen atom as a first manifestation of matter. Ever since then creation has been on its path of expansion, complexity and convergence towards the original state of singularity.

Whatever we discern relates to different material forms or fields of energies. Why it all began and to what end, has been reflected upon and discussed from time immemorial. Philosophers, sages, prophets and scientists reflect and explore meanings and forms to discover relationships and changes due to interactions.

The source and essence of the universe is a mysterious force that permeates whatever is seen and unseen and is referred to as the Divine, the sacred, God, singularity and other names. Countless forces, patterns, laws, designs and self-unfolding programs lead toward the original light, which activates existence. The perceived universe is within limitations of space and time, where all dualities meet and separate, oppose and complement. The essence within this universe is perpetual and self-regulating and is not subject to limitations.

Human beings strive toward wider and deeper sights, insights, knowledge and experiences. We try to connect causes and effects and make sense of dualities in creation. Our spiritual origin propels us to live a meaningful life, which leads to deeper understanding and satisfaction. That is the zone of Oneness – cosmic consciousness, mysterious divine grace, bliss or presence. That is the soul within us.

I. FOUNDATIONS

Emergence

Life began along the shores of oceans in tidal pools many millions of years ago. Much earlier on energy emerged and soon with it its offsprings of matter, forms and cycles of interconnections.

The mystery of this emergence remains veiled from our minds although many useful explanations and descriptions have been discovered. Life and consciousness of it, is the foundation of human existence, experience and our quest.

A wholesome mind has no option other than to accept the challenging gift of life and to try to interact with creation in smooth and natural ways, harmonious with body, mind and heart.

> *The universe and its countless varieties of forms and energies have all emerged from nothingness—an expression of pluralities from unity.*

Dualities & Oneness

The Universe emerged from a mysterious singularity which is incomprehensible to us. Whatever is known and unknown was at origin an intense togetherness, connectedness, inseparability and oneness.

With the emergence of space and time, every type of form and energy emerged in pairs and pluralities. Whatever we discern has its complementary opposite, inseparable from it. Two's are disguised expressions of the One.

Oneness is beyond all values and differentiation, whereas in duality there cannot be any goodness without the seeds of badness. Personal life is accompanied by death and light is discerned due to darkness.

All dualities have their root in the original Oneness to which they return—the Perpetual One.

I. FOUNDATIONS

Self & Soul

Every living entity is sustained by its provider—soul or spirit. Souls differ in their extent of consciousness and thus bodies and minds differ appropriately.

The human soul creates its own evolving self as a companion shadow. From the interplay of self and soul, personality emerges. Mind is an intermediate faculty between the soul and the body that exists through the senses, intelligence and memory.

The soul radiates qualities that are desirable, such as knowledge, life, ability, and numerous other attributes. The self, which carries aspects of its animal connection, desires the soul's qualities and evolves through maturity of mind to spiritual wisdom, culminating in self-discovery, which is soul realization.

It is quite normal for humans to think of themselves as a body/mind identity. The awakened being lives more as a soul.

Form & Meaning

Like all dualities, form and meaning are inseparable, parallel to matter and energy. Every form has its unique characteristics in appearance but in its essence or meaning it can be similar to many other forms.

No two human beings are the same in their outer state, and yet no two human beings are different in their quest for life and its purpose. Everyone struggles towards useful knowledge and contentment.

Most intelligent human beings seek personal understanding of what is visible and is within existence as well as the invisible Reality and Origin.

For every outer there is an inner. All entities emerge from energy and are interconnected in the universe.

I. FOUNDATIONS

Nursery Earth

For all matter, energy and life, there is a beginning and an end. The earth acts like a nursery to produce the human story; every possible existence is given the chance to evolve and grow. Everything in existence interconnects and relates to everything else.

The earth is our birthplace, learning place and burial place. It is where a human being can realize the spiritual origin, the same origin of the universe—the mysterious one Reality.

All imbalances are due to deviations from the direction towards spiritual awareness. The source of all healing is within the original life force questing well-beingness, harmony and balance in body, mind and heart. Our earthly experiences enable us to realize the inseparability between the seen and unseen, body, mind and heart.

> *The origin of earth is celestial and it is the cradle of humanity whose soul is eternal, and whose body and mind are temporal.*

Levels of Consciousness

Consciousness is subtle light or energy that the mind cannot define and delineate its experiences. Life would not be discerned without a basic level of consciousness.

Living plants have rudimentary consciousness and other creatures have greater consciousness, culminating in humans. Within the human experience we discern numerous levels of consciousness, such as physical, mental and subtler aspects.

Human consciousness has the potential to understand characteristics of inert matter and other living entities. The metaphor of Adam being God's responsible steward on earth implies exercising the highest level of consciousness, not disturbing or destroying the natural orders and their direction of evolvement.

> *The first consciousness of a baby relates to touch and suckling. Then come other experiences, culminating in higher consciousness of the soul.*

I. FOUNDATIONS

Attraction & Repulsion

Attractions and repulsions are amongst the major forces that balance life. We are always taking and giving, whether it is air, thought, or other entities.

We are attracted to stability, contentment and harmony and are repulsed by what is considered detrimental to well-beingness.

A child responds with attraction and repulsion for short-term gratification and pleasure. The adult considers longer-term satisfaction. The wise realize that neither attraction nor repulsion brings durable contentment to the heart—the awakened being simply witnesses the changes and remains within the ever constant soul – perfect state of boundlessness.

We are driven to unite with what is attractive to us and are repulsed from what is considered undesirable. The divine source is the cause of all and is ever present at heart.

Evolution & Natural Selection

Creation has been evolving in multi-faceted ways. Energy gave rise to atoms and complex matter such as molecules and living cells. Life is on a trajectory of higher consciousness.

After several hundred million years, today's human mind can comprehend what is beyond the senses. We can imagine and experience what does not exist in material form. Human beings have evolved to straddle the realms of matter and energy.

During the past centuries, we have co-opted natural selection into human programs and objectives—mostly propelled by the illusory idea of progress. Our spiritual nature relates to the advantages of awakening to higher consciousness, not just to creature comfort and ease. Our ecological crisis is rooted in our spiritual undernourishment.

We have all evolved from oneness and are driven to know and experience it through higher consciousness.

I. FOUNDATIONS

Space, Time & Infinitude

In today's world, space has shrunk and we can communicate across the globe instantly. Time, however, remains elusive and everyone considers it the most valuable asset in existence. "Don't waste time, time is money." Thus, we try to save time, be in time. What about the experience of timelessness? No time equates to infinite time.

Personal conditioned life within space and time has emerged from the boundless life force, which exists beyond and within space-time. Human frustration, impatience and anger are due to our souls' celestial nature, caught for a while on earth and confined to space and time. We are animals questing consciousness of infinity, beyond any limitations—ever present. Now. Forever.

To accept natural human limitations and boundaries is the first step towards awareness of the boundless within us—our soul or spirit.

SPECTRUM OF REALITY

Physics & Metaphysics

All materials have physical, chemical and other properties. Living matter also has biological, electromagnetic and other qualities. Scientific discoveries are due to mind, intellect, thought, and creative capacities, illumined by consciousness.

The big questions of: Who am I? Who created life? Where and who is God? Why will nothing completely satisfy any person? Why death? The answers lie in the heart and soul.

These metaphysical issues cannot be fully resolved by mind or reason alone. We need to move from the mental zone to that of higher consciousness beyond thought and identity, which is where physics yields to metaphysics and where supreme consciousness prevails. Metaphysics relates to heart and soul.

We are composed of matter and energy, limited personal consciousness and supreme light. Body and mind function because of soul.

I. FOUNDATIONS

Matter & Energy

From the origin of creation, physical matters and numerous types of energies emerged. These entities lead to the emergence of duality from original unity. They are interconnected and interactive. Energies are mostly invisible and matter is physical and visible.

Matter is energy frozen temporarily as a form and in a specific place. Matter and energy are inseparable companions and share in physical, chemical, electromagnetic and other properties, which combine to bring about specific characteristics and measurable qualities and quantities. They are the earliest plurality that emerged in early creation.

Human thought is an energy that is activated within the brain. Mind and brain demonstrate the connectedness between energy and matter.

Big Bang & Collapse

It is through consciousness that we experience beginnings and ends, in countless ways. Human life on earth has emerged midway between the beginning of creation and its end in a few billion years. Like the stars we are born and then we die. Conception in the womb is like a personal big bang event. Death is the personal-human big collapse.

Higher Consciousness itself is not subject to cycles of beginnings and ends except in relation to personal or conditioned consciousness. Its nature is more subtle and different from all the lights and energies that are discernible. Divine light is not subject to space and time. Neither is the soul.

Every human reflects the story of the universe. However, life itself has no beginning or end. The divine is eternal.

1. FOUNDATIONS

Realities & Reality

Seeking Reality is a major human quest. Anything that is experienced has some Reality from where it draws its energy. That source is permanently Real.

Every experience has some reality, though it is changeable. All that exists within time has its roots within the timeless—Reality. Even a lie has a spark of the Real, which shows its darkness and its extent.

Reality is another name for truth or God. Everything emanates from it and the closer it is to constancy the more it is considered real. All realities begin and end within space and time—Reality pervades all, permeating the universe.

> *Soul is like the holographic representation of the Real. Body and mind are temporary physical representatives of the Real.*

Directional Randomness

In nature, many events appear to be random and are even described as chaotic. Looking at evolution and the ascent of consciousness beginning within life on earth, there seems to be a clear overall direction in life towards its origin – singularity.

The metaphor of the fall of Adam to earth and the need for him to work his way back to heaven alludes to the rise of consciousness towards its cosmic root.

Cycles within smaller scales of space and time may confuse the overall direction in which the universe is moving. When you reflect upon life and read its signs, occasional short-term deviations are insignificant when viewed over a longer period.

The universe follows complex patterns and cycles, many of which are beyond easy comprehension. All emerged from Oneness and are inseparable from that state.

I. FOUNDATIONS

Normal & Unusual

We are naturally at ease with what we know and are familiar. That connection is considered normal and acceptable. Yet we always seek new experiences to enrich our senses and mind through sound, sight, smell, touch and taste.

We love to explore what is beyond the horizons. Creativity and discoveries come to those who seek the unusual or rare. The most valued precious stone is the rarest. The ultimate and rarest gem of all is the soul and the consciousness that it provides. To know the soul is to go beyond all knowledge that is based on mind and brain. Spiritual knowledge arises due to connections between the light of the soul and supreme consciousness – the rarely awakened to but ever present.

We seek stability and normality but our spirit belongs to the eternal undefinable.

Religion & Belief

The spirit of Adam was born in the quantum field of Oneness and infinitude. The descent of Adam to earth is the prelude to ascension from dualities back to original Oneness – ever present.

Humans emerged with the evolvement of consciousness and the experience of connectedness between the finite and infinite. We live within this mysterious reality where the transient and the eternal are inseparable. To explain this situation is the origin of most religions.

Within every human being is a drive and quest to realize and experience perpetual oneness of essence. Belief is an expression of the hope to resonate with this Truth whilst in earthly transition.

Most religions propose cosmic Oneness that permeates the universe. The tangible world emanates and returns to the One. The soul knows this truth.

I. FOUNDATIONS

Saints & Villains

Higher consciousness and our soul is the source of everything we experience. In the past, people specialized in religious, spiritual or philosophical issues that could guide them to more stable and better living.

Monasteries and other special environments were provided for people with an inclination towards understanding and unison with higher consciousness. Villains and criminals, however, were common amongst the masses and whenever caught, were isolated to reduce their damage to others—punishment by disconnection. Saints often chose isolation or disconnection from normal life.

Sainthood and villainhood represent the two extreme levels of conduct and consciousness. It is the extent, duration and purpose of seclusion that determined the labels of saint or villain.

> *Deviant behaviour can be destructive and dark, whereas within every heart lies the perfect light and pathway to enlightenment.*

Knowledge & Love

Knowledge is a field of energy that brings about connectedness at the physical, material, mental and spiritual levels. Rationality and intellect are the agents of earthly knowledge and demonstrate it. Love is a field that connects and unites matter or energy where there is no previous apparent relationship.

All physical affinities, chemical reactions and countless other subtle forces can be affected by Love. From the start of creation, the power of Love has been operating to connect and relate what was initially gathered in pre-creational density and togetherness: One.

Love is the cosmic force that constantly appears in different ways. It is the force that holds together the entire universe.

> *To love someone is the first step to experiencing the divine attributes. Knowledge is a force that unifies.*

I. FOUNDATIONS

Justice & Injustice

The root of justice is in the Reality of Oneness and injustice describes the perceived distance from perfect unity. Divine justice is not relative and, in truth, there is none other than that Reality.

Injustice begins with the perception of human separation and independence from Oneness. Then we experience otherness, personal identity, and biography. Each human being is like a particle, which is only there temporarily due to its perpetual spiritual origin.

Justice is to acknowledge and live in resonance with origin. Injustice is the illusion and identification with personal and conditioned consciousness boxed within space and time. To realize the inherent injustice within our humanity is the first great step to transcend to the lights of divinity. Therein lies the just path.

*When you identify with your
biography, ego, or lower self,
you are doing yourself injustice.
The soul radiates divine justice.*

Happiness & Misery

Happiness relates to stability, contentment, tranquillity and inner peace. These are the result of consciousness of Oneness and experiential connectedness and continuity. When the mind is still and desires less and the heart beams its light of soul consciousness, elevation in spirit and cheerfulness becomes tangible.

Misery is disturbance, discord, pain, fear, and constant change in desires and attachments. All our senses lead to concepts and ideas of the mind whereas sustained happiness lies beyond the mind, and is not dependant on the dynamics that take place within space and time. It is full presence in the moment.

Turning away from thoughts and expectations and pursuing the map of Reality will lead to soul realisation and the ever-present garden of inner delights and insights. There is no misery in that domain.

The soul is beyond changes that the self experiences. To live as a soul in the moment leads to experiencing the pure thrill of life.

I. FOUNDATIONS

Balance & Rationality

The human soul provides life to body and mind. It is through the mind that we can live in the world of dualities whilst energized by unity. We are caught in between.

With maturity, the mind develops its rationality, reasoning and knowledge of causality and connectedness. Humanity functions within the limitations of space and time and the cycles of appearance and disappearance. The primal light of the soul beams fairness, balance, and other forces that drive towards the intended destiny—witnessing perfection.

It is through higher intellect that we can bring about some order to the challenges of the world of change. The love for balance is due to the fact that every moment is balanced between the eternal now and the experience of change.

Your soul is the source of life, fairness and wisdom. It is timeless and independent of all change. Intellect and contemplation lead to the soul.

War & Peace

It is in human nature to love peace, stillness and silence. Aggression and violence are the dark side of that nature. Peace lies within our heart and is the condition of our soul, and is disturbed when thought arises in the mind – distraction from pure consciousness.

Human development requires the senses to excite thought, curiosity and incite mental challenges. The nature of duality is to create difference, discord and the sense of otherness.

Inner and outer war, are indicators of the lack of realization of peace within the heart, where the soul resides. We can enter that home only after leaving behind all judgements and thoughts. World peace will follow when individuals discover their own inner joyful peace. Turn away from chaos, you experience order.

Peace is a by-product of an individual's discovery of joy and tranquillity. It is the soul's nature and the quest of reflective humans.

I. FOUNDATIONS

Wealth & Poverty

There are two zones of poverty and wealth. One is the outer material world, where more is more until it reaches its natural limits. The other is inner wealth and contentment. Outer poverty can cause temporary misery and hardship and inner poverty can cause gloom and depression.

Inner wealth is the condition of a contented heart, where the soul resides. Inner poverty is due to a weak link between body, mind and heart. A healthy life is based on a balance between outer and inner contentment and satisfaction.

The self or ego is the changing shadow, which asserts its presence. As for the soul, it is the centre of wealth, balance and goodness and exudes those lights. As such, every human being carries the essence of infinite wealth (soul) and abject poverty (animal self).

> *The sense of wealth lies within the soul. Outer poverty is a drive towards gaining wealth outwardly (never enough) or inwardly or both.*

Quantity & Quality

Whatever is discernible has a particular quality and quantity, which interact, complement each other, and change.

When a certain quality of an entity becomes extensive and increases in prevalence, a point is reached where it changes. When generosity becomes common and ordinary, it loses its quality of a special virtue. Equally, when something becomes very rare and is least available, it becomes valued and desirable.

In human life we quest for what is considered good in qualities and in greater quantities. We seek wealth or knowledge beyond need or necessity. The human soul contains all the desirable qualities beyond measure. It belongs to boundlessness and timeless consciousness.

Whatever we consider good we like to increase in quality and quantity. Whatever we dislike, we hope will diminish in quantity and quality.

I. FOUNDATIONS

Obsession & Passion

The mind quests for discoveries and knowledge. The child interacts with creation and is excited with its exploration and new experiences.

This human drive is an expression of the self's obsession with its life source, the soul. Human mind, identity and ego are shadows caused by the light of the soul. Like a moth, the self is drawn incessantly to that light.

Different types and degrees of obsession are variations of the original self-soul link. The primal drive of all senses is to unite and be at One. Outer obsessions with objects or relationships are reflections of the innate obsession of self with soul – the soul mate.

> *Humanity is obsessed with its original nature—divinity and singularity. That is the root of all desires, passions and obsessions.*

Quest For The Best

'The best' is a relative term that applies to changing circumstances as well as to that which is more durable. We are naturally driven to what is considered best. It implies satisfaction, pleasantness, hope and goodness. All of these lights and feelings emanate from the heart and soul.

Ultimately, the best relates to a durable inner state that is the source of contentment and delight. Outer happiness for everyone is most unlikely as someone's pleasure may be another's misery.

The quest for excellence and perfection emanates from the soul, whose nature and state is divine perfection, and is the goal of existence. There lies the root of quest for the best.

> *The human being quests for the best all the time. This force is beamed constantly from the soul.*

I. FOUNDATIONS

Human Mirroring

All human souls are of the same composition. Everyone is born alone and will die alone, but cannot live without other human beings. Our connectedness and relationships are due to our souls, minds and neuron circuitries. The more we exercise our mirror neurons, the more we experience empathy and connectedness with others and at higher and subtler levels of consciousness until soul resonance prevails.

The state of a soul is constant whereas our minds and bodies are in continuous change and flux. Empathy is part of the ascent of consciousness towards its origin and source. Humanity is One whilst it is experienced in duality, diversity and otherness. Divinity is One. You strive to the One—integrated.

> *We desire certainty and contentment and fear the unknown. We mirror each other in fears, hopes and other emotions.*

Power Of The Gaze

A baby's life and consciousness is enhanced by the mother's attention and affection. With the human gaze, a photon becomes a particle and acts differently from its wave field. Thus develops a baby's self-awareness.

Consciousness is like other invisible powers: we know its effect, its different levels and intensities, but we do not know its exact nature and how it affects us. Light and sight are similarly mysterious. The mother-child relationship is like putting light to a candle. The baby is like a fresh wick, the mother's gaze sets it alight. The growing child yearns for parents and others to acknowledge its presence. It loves to be watched and looked at. The more attention it gets the more confident it becomes. Human sight has a normal quality as well as a mysterious one. Science has not resolved the effect of eyesight upon the double slit experiment when a photon changes from particle to wave.

The spectrum of our consciousness stretches from limitlessness to the physical and human sight adds a new dimension.

I. FOUNDATIONS

Why?

Every why is an attempt to connect. Why do we love light? It connects us with the surrounding area and enables us to move and act more efficiently. Why do we love? In order to connect more deeply. Why do you want to hear someone's voice or meet him or her? Why do you want to connect? In order to widen your knowledge and conscious experience. Why do you continue? Because the light of the soul within you is eternal.

Every why comes back to one of the three roots: to increase consciousness, through connectedness, and continuity. The whys will eventually lead to the domain of Oneness. It is the divine trick to reveal itself – eternally present but veiled.

> *A question is the mental excuse needed to receive the gift of the answer that was already begging the question.*

2. Nature of Existence

SPECTRUM OF EXISTENCE

- One-Two-One
- Balanced Dualities
- Perfection Of Dualities
- Two Zones Of Reality
- Quest For Origin
- Passion For Life
- Earthly Transition
- Microbes, Insects & Animals
- Stability Of Change
- Cycles Of Birth & Death
- Body, Mind & Soul
- Identity, Thought & Time
- Mental Occupation
- More, Less & Beyond
- Endless Lights & Shadows
- Alienation & Integration
- Small, Big & In-Between
- Knowledge & Understanding
- Provision For Soul & Body

SPECTRUM OF REALITY

- ✠ Metamorphosis
- ✠ Action & Reaction
- ✠ Fear & Hope
- ✠ Tough But Gentle
- ✠ Duty-Bound Liberation
- ✠ Will & Action
- ✠ Comic Tragedy
- ✠ Illusion Of Success
- ✠ Failed Victory
- ✠ Survival Of The Fittest
- ✠ Oasis In The Desert
- ✠ Angels
- ✠ Elementals

Introduction

Many human concerns relate to the state of body, mind and senses. We hope for good health, comfort, ease and growth. We also desire to have a clear and cheerful mind, yet life's experiences swing between difficulty and ease, good and bad and other uncertainties.

Whatever exists, visible or invisible, comes in pairs that appear as opposites whilst in reality they are inseparable. The early stars were born in the cosmic soup inferno. Then they continued the path of interaction whilst evolving and changing in time and space. Cycles and patterns of emergence, evolvement, growth and disintegration linked and mingled, engulfing all entities and energies. Whatever begins will also end and whatever emerges will submerge.

The drive for survival propels living creatures to look for ways and means for sustenance and propagation. Increase and expansion simply echo the origin of creation. The nature of human existence is to be aware, witness and experience balance, stability, and mental and intellectual evolvement. Purposefulness and a sense of meaning and achievement give life hope and enthusiasm. The primal purpose is to witness the beauty, majesty and perfection of The Cosmic Spirit — ever-present as the human soul.

Conscious creations desire wider and deeper knowledge, power and full consciousness. The human limitations of personal consciousness take us to the edge of cosmic consciousness itself. Our earthly existence is a prelude to the realization of our celestial reality. Once we experience the limitations of space and time, we are driven toward the

SPECTRUM OF REALITY

original state of singularity and oneness. This is the story of the descent and ascent of Adam and his offspring. Once on earth we are driven to experience boundless horizons.

2. NATURE OF EXISTENCE

One-Two-One

The universe emerged from a single origin—a mysterious Oneness which permeates all. From the earliest stages in creation countless entities emerged, propelled along a course of complexity and evolvement.

From the One, dualities and pluralities emerge, only to develop, mature and then subside back to Oneness. The tree of life with its roots and trunk produces multiple branches and expressions. The entire universe is a manifestation of a Divine Reality beyond the mind's capacity to fully understand.

For thousands of years this entity was called God, or self-created being, or Brahman, Allah and so on. Singularity is one of several new modern names, so is the Absolute and Reality.

Reality is One and it manifests as countless entities within space and time, each carrying a reminder of the origin.

Balanced Dualities

Life emanates from a source whose qualities are in complete balance and perfection. This is the sacred Oneness from where all dualities emerge. All of our experiences in life, through our senses, faculties of cognition and consciousness are polar and contain complementary opposites.

Every pleasure is associated with a potential pain. Only after transcending these dualities to higher consciousness may we experience the zone of unity and Oneness.

The challenge of life is to learn and read the maps of dualities and how all opposites balance and neutralize each other. What is real is original Oneness—Ever perfect.

Reflecting upon dualities and opposites one may discern their origin of Oneness at source.

2. NATURE OF EXISTENCE

Perfection Of Dualities

All dualities are two sides of the same coin; their root and destination is one and a clear reflective mind can discover this truth. They are qualities that emanate from one source, like a rose which has a physical form and fragrance— two qualities from one entity.

When you view pluralities through the lens of Oneness, you experience beauty, majesty and perfection. In themselves, dualities compete for dominance and prevalence until peace and neutrality emerge. They interact and then balance out.

Whatever you experience is only half the picture. Look for the complementary opposite and you will get the full story.

Two Zones Of Reality

Whatever we experience emerges from and subsides into the universal pool of energy and matter. Change is continuous in the universe whose essence is constant.

Every aspect of consciousness and life emanates from a higher zone of consciousness and original source. Our experiences are transient and yet we always seek constancy and perpetuity – The Real.

The permanent Reality we seek is within our soul and is connected to the Cosmic Soul. Unless we experience this Truth, frustration, depression, and sadness are likely to emerge.

Whatever change we experience has emerged from the original state of pure consciousness and Oneness.

2. NATURE OF EXISTENCE

Quest For Origin

The present moment is the most potent and powerful link to the essence of time. We are habitually distracted from facing the immensity of now. In our quest to understand the meaning of life and existence, we search for origins. Our interest in ancestral roots is one aspect of this primal drive.

We ask when, why, and how life began. Plausible answers transcend the intellect and causality. They are heart-felt. Religious people use myths, legends and metaphors such as 'God's will' and 'God's command'.

The curiosity for origins remains a drawing force at all times. You can say it is the quest for God—the originator, the ever-present but not visible or definable. Our soul transmits this Truth.

It is natural to seek the knowledge of our beginning, which may give indication of the meaning and direction of life.

Passion For Life

Life makes us conscious of interdependence with other creations and entities. We are obsessed with longevity and continuity. This love and obsession for life is the foundation of all human interests and quests. It is because of consciousness that we understand attraction, repulsion, cause and effect, relationship dynamics and the desire for greater knowledge and well-beingness. Love for life is the root of all quests.

Personal life as associated with birth and death is a representation or sample of life itself, which is cosmic and eternal. The highest point of human love is life itself. Respect for another human being's life is a respect for this most valued gift in existence. Passion for life adds potency to everyday living.

Love of life points towards the understanding of all intricate relationships as it manifests on earth or elsewhere. Passion for life is love of its perpetual essence.

2. NATURE OF EXISTENCE

Earthly Transition

It is natural for us to be apprehensive, concerned and hopeful about the future. We seek well-beingness, ease, and expect continuous improvement and richness of our life's quality.

From ancient times, several cultures and religions promoted the idea that human beings are celestial lights passing through the earth in order to realize the connectedness between heavens and earth. Our body and soul are the connections.

Our earthly life entails some training and exercise of choice to restrict egotistic veils and distractions and to enhance awakening to the truth of real and durable human reality—heart and soul.

> *Most people complain that time flies, but the awakened ones discover the inner zone of timelessness.*

… SPECTRUM OF REALITY …

Microbes, Insects & Animals

Life appeared on earth a long time ago along the seashores and tidal pools. Then microbial life began to replicate itself and multiply, mimicking continuity and eternal presence. In time, numerous lives multiplied in form and complexity leading to various vegetation and then insects and countless other creatures evolving in consciousness and complexity. Numerous species of animals appeared surpassing the consciousness and intelligence of previous ones.

Hominids seems to be the culmination of the animal stage of evolution leading to present day human beings with a frontal lobe that enables transcendence of all limitations of consciousness. The human being is considered responsible for safeguarding and protecting the natural environment—a sort of steward on earth, not a plunderer.

Humanity carries traces of life's origin and all evolutionary steps physically, mentally and spiritually.

2. NATURE OF EXISTENCE

Stability Of Change

All human experiences are subject to change within space and time. The speed and extent of change refers to the intensity and the rapidity of sensory perceptions. When everything is absolutely still and one is thoughtless, time seems to stop and we are at the gate of timelessness. Peace is at the edge of space and time. It is still, stable and constant. Life began from a zone of singularity and perfect stability. When creation began to manifest that original absolute stability gave into change, dynamic interactions and multitudinous manifestations.

The self always longs for change for its evolvement and destiny towards its soul. The constant soul is the source of the self that enables it to experience change. The soul is ever stable and the self is ever changing.

We experience change and movement due to the stable nature of our soul.

Cycles Of Birth & Death

Human consciousness is potentially wider and deeper than that of most animals. Personal life is framed between birth and death, whereas life as such is not limited. That perception and experience is a big challenge to all.

The entire universe interacts according to countless patterns and cycles, which include human life. Limited consciousness leads towards higher consciousness by transcending limitations. Fear of death helps to ensure care for personal life and to prolong it. When the mind stops and inner peace and silence prevail, then the experience of boundless life may override the habitual notion of identity, mind and limitation. Awakening to complete consciousness breaks the illusions of mental habits and identity—full evolvement.

With reflection we experience numerous patterns representing connection between matter and energy. Human life is a sample of perpetual life.

2. NATURE OF EXISTENCE

Body, Mind & Soul

The mystery of creation drives us towards its discovery. Science, philosophy and spiritual pursuits are attempts to widen and deepen our consciousness and knowledge. This mystery is due to the ever-present source of Oneness from which all dualities emerge. We naturally differentiate between matter, body, and the domain of the mind, senses, memory, feelings and emotions. The mystery of life is as wide as the universe itself.

Each part of our human composition has distinct characteristics but they all connect and communicate. The quest for harmony and well-beingness leads to discoveries, knowledge and closeness to the unifying field of Reality, which is not limited to our identity and part-time life on earth. Our soul is the resident agent of Cosmic Spirit.

> *The reflective person deals holistically with body, mind and soul. Purity of heart is necessary for the soul's light to reveal the map of Reality.*

Identity, Thought & Time

We always look for meaning or purpose in the world of action or thought. The ultimate purpose of human life is to experience the infinitude of life itself and dwell therein. There lies perpetual light and complete consciousness.

The feeling of separation is at the root of personal identity and spiritual constriction. Nature and nurture produce thought that gives rise to earthly authorship of personal identity and the illusion of independence.

Time and space are the frames in which identity is given a temporary virtual reality which draws its energy from the one Reality.

Every being develops certain characteristics which give it a separate identity. To experience the Real we need to transcend all mental constructs.

2. NATURE OF EXISTENCE

Mental Occupation

The mind connects the physical world with subtle energy fields and spiritual forces. From our early years we develop memories and experiences which become more complex within consciousness and this may help us to live a more contented life.

We are habit-forming creatures and therefore our patterns of thoughts tend to repeat and dominate. We are occupied by our past and hope for a better future. Many of us are handicapped by previous suppressed, negative and restrictive experiences. To tap into the life source we need to transcend the mind and practice mindfulness, silence and oblivion.

The mind operates at numerous levels including that of sleepwalking. Fulfilment is durable when mind and heart resonate.

More, Less & Beyond

The mind measures, relates, compares and concludes. We seek increase and desire more but we also experience loss, limitations and unfulfilled desires: Perpetual uncertainty.

Our soul and higher consciousness is not subject to limitation and defined measures. Qualities and quantities of anything relate to conditioned consciousness and earthly identity. Supreme consciousness is boundless and free from all limitations of space and time. In our conditioned consciousness more is more, but less is more as we quest higher consciousness. In that zone of boundlessness there are no measures or entities—primal perfect presence.

> *Human nature wants to measure, evaluate and attract what is desirable. Complete consciousness is beyond all.*

2. NATURE OF EXISTENCE

Endless Lights & Shadows

We can imagine the start of the universe as being primal original light. The terms sacred, divine energy, or source, are also used to indicate that. From that original universal essence arose endless varieties of lights, energies and matter. Within space and time everything that appears comes with its twin; this is the realm of dualities. Thus, every light is accompanied by its shadow. They emerge from the fountain of mysteries on a trajectory to return to origin—at peace and complete.

Light is a widely experienced energy and comes in countless qualities and quantities, accompanied by shadows.

Everything that we experience is one of many beams of light that permeates the universe.

Alienation & Integration

Negative emotions and the feeling of separation, individual identity, movement and change are the cause of most of our confusions and difficulties. Occasionally we feel like aliens on earth and have to cope with insecurity, fears and other physical and mental concerns.

We yearn for a reliable and welcoming home and for friendships and connectedness that make us feel secure and happy. When the mind is subservient to the soul within the heart, a sense of stability and integration will take root. This unison is essential for a sustainable state of wholesomeness – head and heart in balance.

> *By transcending the mind, you experience integration and balanced well-beingness – your soul's perfection.*

2. NATURE OF EXISTENCE

Small, Big & In-Between

The universe is made up of infinitesimally small entities and imperceptible energies as well as vast galactic masses. Quantum mechanics is at one end of the spectrum and astrophysics at the other end. Human position and perception is in the middle—a microcosm that reflects the macrocosm.

The human desire to know and understand everything is indicative of the potential within us that knows all. The drive, mystery and reality of human life in embedded within the soul. By our mind and heart we can imagine and understand the micro as well as the mega.

With the senses and mind we can measure and relate to quality and quantity. The light of the soul takes us to boundlessness.

Knowledge & Understanding

Knowledge is an energy field that illumines and describes what encounters it. It connects cause, effect and relationships that can be understood due to its light. As we begin to understand the outer and inner meaning of a situation, the mind expands and experiences satisfaction and contentment. Intelligence is sharpened.

Knowledge is at numerous levels. It encompasses minute entities and realities as well as realities of immense dimensions. Human senses and perception are in the middle of this wide range. Spiritual knowledge transcends the mind and relates to supreme consciousness and realities contained therein.

Contentment and happiness relate to connectedness through knowledge that transcends mind, senses and beyond— the lights of the soul. There, knowledge and love meet.

2. NATURE OF EXISTENCE

Provision For Soul & Body

Sometimes what we think to be the cause is in fact the effect. Sometimes dualities play tricks with the mind. It is often thought that spiritual practices and prayers are for the soul and physical food is for the body. The reverse is truer.

Spiritual practices are for the benefit of the body, for that is where the soul resides and provides its heavenly nourishment. Physical food is for the soul's sake which provides life for the body which needs food for its maintenance.

Awareness of what and how we eat is a spiritual act in essence.

> *The constant human challenge is to maintain the balance between our sensory world and the inner light of the soul.*

Metamorphosis

Our complex and diversified life on earth is the result of millions of years of adaptation, mutation and metamorphosis. Creation provides countless metaphors regarding our inner life and spiritual evolution.

The prickly looking caterpillar will transform into an amazing, beautiful butterfly. The same surprising gap exists between our normal human condition and the soul that is beyond all limitations and shortcomings.

When the human caterpillar is touched by grace, it may metamorphose. We are evolving at all times towards higher consciousness and may realize the magnificent soul and its light —sacred presence within the heart.

> *Our resident butterfly is the soul within. The intellect and higher quest is the pathway to metamorphosis, which we label as enlightenment.*

2. NATURE OF EXISTENCE

Action & Reaction

Anything that exists as form or energy relates to cause and effect. Human thoughts, intentions and actions follow the same pattern. We live in a universe of receivers and transmitters, which are interconnected in an obvious, as well as a deeper and indiscernible sense.

Any movement or change in the physical or mental state has its repercussion. Every thought or intention can result in a desirable outcome or regrets and guilt. Movement is along the path of higher consciousness and spiritual evolvement or random. The higher is the value of intention, the more beneficial will be its outcome. There is no escape from this design.

The intentions behind your actions, as well as the appropriateness of the action, will determine the ultimate outcome and its impact.

Fear & Hope

Quite often we are optimistic and hopeful about our future well-beingness. We prefer hope and optimism to fear and gloom. We hope to grow in experience and wisdom, and to attain our desires and expectations. We act and engage in activities that we consider will improve our lives.

All hopes however are irrevocably wedded to fear; the same goes for pleasure and pain. Fear of pain and failure can enhance caution and attention to direction and action.

We live between fear and hope. We are inspired by hope and hesitant due to fear. Our soul only radiates perfections.

2. NATURE OF EXISTENCE

Tough But Gentle

Soft is balanced by hard and tough by gentle. These complementary opposites are experienced most of the time as either/or. In the subtler world of energies and patterns they are complementary, rather than exclusive. Good and bad are born as inseparable twins.

Attitudes towards a situation are often experienced as gentle or forceful, immediate or delayed.

Low level pressure applied over a long period can be more effective than forcing a situation which may not be sustainable. Force will flow smoothly when applied along the course of natural tendency.

> *Your soul is the most gentle as well as most powerful and tough. It is not subject to change.*

Duty-Bound Liberation

Normal consciousness is limited and conditioned. It derives its energy from boundless supreme consciousness. To respond appropriately to our human limitations and drives, we need to awaken to higher levels of consciousness. Our humanity includes numerous levels and intensities of connectedness, empathy and interactive dynamics.

The sense of duty and higher human values can override the selfish and whimsical self. Friendship, loyalty, selfless acts and other human links may help the evolvement from the animal self towards our soul. It is only through transcendence of body and mind that we experience lasting liberation – perpetual awareness of Reality.

To acknowledge and perform one's ethical and spiritual duties is to be close to transcending the limitations of the self and human identity.

2. NATURE OF EXISTENCE

Will & Action

Young people enjoy an active life driven by rewards of discoveries and achievements. For much of our life, we are engaged in activities aimed to reduce our needs and desires, which naturally continue. We strive towards peace and yet we continue to add more expectations, attachments and desires!

An intention may lead to a will, attention and action. In all situations it is aimed to bring ease, comfort and peace. Awakening to higher consciousness, inner intention becomes clearer. So will the plan of action.

The enlightened person has few personal desires and needs. These will be fulfilled with least personal effort. The soul has no needs or desires: it is perpetually fulfilled.

Our spiritual growth is landmarked by clear intentions, efficient action and regular contemplation. From hesitancy comes clarity.

SPECTRUM OF REALITY

Comic Tragedy

It is a relief and a delight when you are out of a difficult challenge or an affliction. The good news that replaces fear and anxiety is cause for smiles and cheerfulness. When relieved from a feared tragedy we may even laugh and celebrate the passing of a dreadful experience that has passed without damage.

All our disappointments are transient and short-lived. As humans we relate to what disturbs our body, mind or emotions. The soul is the constant light that illumines the changes recognized by the self or ego. Access to the soul's light is by transcendence of the mind and identity. The soul is the greatest treasure there is—all become insignificant when seen through its lens.

Relief and humour replace fear and afflictions when events are witnessed as passing shadows projected upon the soul.

2. NATURE OF EXISTENCE

Illusion Of Success

Human consciousness is between no consciousness and supreme consciousness. With respect to emotions, feelings and judgements, the healthy human state recognizes the balance between good, bad, and other dualities and influences.

Success implies a desire or an ambition fulfilled. Our life's journey is punctuated by drives to quieten the mind, which occurs at points of success. We are obsessed by the need to quieten the mind, but continuously introduce new thoughts. The experience of success is a tranquil and contented mind.

Disturbing our inner peace due to new ideas and projects until we follow the path of mindfulness and transcendence: there lies real success due to soul's access.

Awakening is to go beyond success and failure, past the dark side of success which seeds future failures.

Failed Victory

From childhood, characters and personal qualities develop and evolve by the interaction of nurture and nature. The self loves to be witnessed and seen to be doing well. We seek success and being special.

To achieve what is desirable and be admired is considered a good 'norm', yet life's experiences are a balance between success and failure, acceptance and rejection—a zero sum outcome.

Constant victory is a state within higher consciousness where everything is part of the oceanic unity and perpetuity. This is the zone of spirits or souls and perfect beingness.

> *The soul is beyond the idea of failure or success. Self is the soul's shadow on earth that experiences duality and quests for unity – victory.*

2. NATURE OF EXISTENCE

Survival Of The Fittest

Survival and evolvement on earth requires fitness at several levels and the ability to adapt to change. A few millennia ago, fitness meant physical strength and power. More recently, it meant mental power and the ability to control, manipulate or outsmart others.

For spiritual seekers, fitness implies the ability to transcend body, mind and senses into a zone of higher consciousness and lights. Nowadays survival of the fittest implies a healthy body, a clear mind, a pure heart, and skills and talents that are in demand. As we are both material and spiritual entities, we need skills and fitness at the body, mind and heart levels. The ultimate fitness is to live as a soul. That is perfection.

The fit and wholesome person is in this world, but not swamped or afflicted by adversity, fear and sorrow. The soul is eternally perfect.

Oasis In The Desert

The illumined heart of the awakened being is like an oasis in the desert of human life. No one is spared from the grace of challenges and difficulties. This is how the invisible light of the cosmic master points us toward the inner oasis.

The conscientious human being wants to share the goodness and joys of life with others whilst there are invariably disappointments, difficulties and regrets. We often feel a thirst for revitalising water and the need for fresh air—both materially and spiritually. Paradise is not only in the hereafter, it is already in our heart— our oasis and inner sanctum. Outer gardens and beautiful vistas are samples of the divine perfect garden.

When you discover that bliss that emanates from your own soul, you are awakening to the Divine promise.

2. NATURE OF EXISTENCE

Angels

There are numerous creations in existence beside humanity. Angels are varied in nature and power. They have specific directions and purpose, whose effects sometimes manifest and at most other times do not.

Seers, shamans and prophets have mentioned encounters with angels as both discernible entities as well as invisible. The idea of having a personal guardian angel may partially relate to the light of the soul and not an outer angel.

Guidance and authority for everyone, comes from their inner soul when awakened to it, otherwise discontentment and distraction prevail. Angels are considered agents of goodness and their opposite dark forces are referred to as Satan or evil forces.

> *The human soul has higher potential than angels do. It is sacred and is entangled with the cosmic soul.*

Elementals

There are numerous other beings or entities which are unseen, but their effect is felt by us. The Djinn, for example, are based on fire and smoke in contrast to the human constituents of earth, water and light. There are some similarities between us and many of these 'elementals'. These beings may live in groups, families, tribes and nations. Amongst them are good beings evolving towards higher consciousness as well as those who cause mischief and degradation. Access to deceased person's souls and mediumship are also examples of connections in consciousness.

Some human beings connect with Djinn or similar forces and are able to harness them up to a point. The outcome is often regrettable as these are not predictable and follow different paths of life to ours.

> *Djinn are the imperceptible versions of human beings with similar patterns of life and death.*

3. Consciousness

SPECTRUM OF CONSCIOUSNESS

- ✠ Womb Of Space & Time
- ✠ Deaf & Dumb
- ✠ Self-Awareness & Higher Consciousness
- ✠ Conditioned & Full Consciousness
- ✠ Spectrum Of Consciousness
- ✠ Ascent Of Consciousness
- ✠ Flashes Of Higher Consciousness
- ✠ Shadows Of Consciousness
- ✠ Living Consciousness
- ✠ Types Of Intelligence
- ✠ Awakened, Illumined & Enlightened
- ✠ Life Is Now
- ✠ Constantly Changeable
- ✠ Grey, Black & White
- ✠ Quest For Paradise
- ✠ Outer & Inner Awareness
- ✠ Asset & Liability Of Memory
- ✠ Root Of Exaggeration

SPECTRUM OF REALITY

- ✠ Suffering & Liberation
- ✠ Competition To Cooperation
- ✠ Dreams

Introduction

Life is discerned via consciousness. Human consciousness spans a very wide spectrum of experiencing and understanding of realities. Consciousness may be defined as an energy field or light that generates other subtle forces such as intelligence, knowledge's, understandings, feelings, emotions and other mental and spiritual states.

Like colours that emanate from visible light, consciousness produces many discernible qualities such as love, generosity and other attributes, both high and low. We are conscious of the positive effect of kindness and empathy and shun enmity and discordance—we prefer connection.

It is in human nature to have a clear and sharp mind and to understand and relate to what is happening around us. We are driven towards stability, balance and peace and to connect our inner world, of body and mind, to the outer world. We receive and transmit signals, signs and other complex visible or subtle linguistic expressions.

We continuously seek self-sustained joy and goodness. We quest for eternal life, beyond our personal, conditioned and limited life. The biography of consciousness begins with basic life within the tidal pools of lakes and oceans. The simple chemistry of earth, water and sun was energized alchemically and gave the first cells their life—the birth of consciousness.

We are driven to experience connectedness and continuity in what gives us stability, pleasure or happiness. The dynamics of human nature are based on the interplay between the eternal soul within us and its shadow companion, the lower self. Initially we think we are in charge and can choose our own intentions or actions. The fortunate few realize that what was in charge throughout was a holographic representation of supreme reality –the cosmic soul – the soul within the heart.

3. CONSCIOUSNESS

Womb Of Space & Time

As everything else in existence is balanced in dualities, so is the twin of space and time where all of creation was conceived and is evolving to its ultimate destiny.

Every human being is a composite of light or spirit, which brings about sentiency to earthly matter and energies within space and time.

After being ejected from the womb of Oneness, the newborn experiences a wider and complex environment and earthly consciousness. Through awakening and enlightenment to the infinitude of soul consciousness within us, we are born again—returning to the original state.

Life and death are experienced in two zones, one biological and the other one spiritual, beyond the confines of space and time.

Deaf & Dumb

Cosmic consciousness is filtered, modified and reduced in quality and quantity, in order to energize the mind. The baby begins with a basic flicker of awareness and as its brain develops its capacity for higher consciousness increases until full maturity. Personal consciousness draws its energy from higher consciousness and aspires to it.

Few people experience aspects of higher consciousness, often referred to as intuition, insights, epiphanies or other descriptions alluding to the unusual or the special. Most people live and die with limited conditioned consciousness. A sleepwalker too has consciousness but within greater limitations. All of us have the potential to be illumined by a much higher level of awareness, but the capacity to do so is diminished by other defects of mind and intellect—most are metaphorically deaf and dumb. The innate potential is there but the physical, chemical, mental limitations may be so severe they do not manifest as such.

> *It is a natural drive in us to go beyond any limitations that we perceive, but many of us do not have the capacity or drive.*

3. CONSCIOUSNESS

Self-Awareness & Higher Consciousness

Self-awareness begins with taste, sound, smell and other physical and sensory experiences. Then come feelings, emotions, thoughts, likes, dislikes, and values shaped by personal needs, culture and habit.

Shyness, guilt and other emotions are related to subtler aspects of mind and its unconscious orientation. The quest for peace, tranquillity and peace of mind, are simple indicators of an inner drive to tap into higher consciousness within our soul. That is the ultimate goal of awakened beings – to be illumined and enlightened.

The arc of the ascent of consciousness begins at the physical level along a path connecting to supreme consciousness.

Conditioned & Full Consciousness

Human life is defined by the limitations of time and space, whereas the soul belongs to the zone of boundlessness. It is natural for human beings to struggle to be free from all restrictions and boundaries. We are obsessed with the free spirit.

Conditioned consciousness stimulates us towards higher consciousness from which we draw energy. We are connected to this consciousness and we seek it as our sustaining lifeline. Our reality is pure consciousness which is modified through human limitations and habits.

Higher aspirations and quests are descriptions of what is transmitted from the soul's complete consciousness.

> *Personal awareness of life is the starting point of experiencing life in its infinite boundless reality.*

3. CONSCIOUSNESS

Spectrum Of Consciousness

Consciousness can produce a discernible response to a stimulation that has been received by a conscious subject. Life is experienced as discernible outcome of consciousness. A human being loses consciousness and dies when the brain and heart stop functioning.

At the foundation of human consciousness lie our nervous and sensory systems of sight, hearing, touch, smell and taste. Then we experience numerous levels and types of feelings and emotions, which affect our physical state.

Much of the health of the body depends on the quality and the health of the mind and emotions. All levels of our consciousness, as well as the subconscious, derive their power from higher consciousness, which flows from the soul, which in turn transmits its spectrum of universal lights and energies.

Spiritual evolvement relates to higher consciousness of our soul. The spectrum of consciousness encompasses our humanity and divinity.

Ascent Of Consciousness

We experience time along a direction. We have a memory of some past, a certain awareness of the present, and hope for a better future. Life and consciousness began many million years ago and continued to evolve and grow in complexity. Every living entity with a consciousness seems to strive towards a higher level of consciousness.

Several world religions use the metaphor of the descent of Adam as a prelude to ascension. We want to know what is beyond limits—the domain of pure consciousness and our spirit. Adam desired the knowledge of the eternal and the descent to earthly temporality is like the preparation for return to the immortality of the soul in a paradise state.

The constant human quest to know, connect, and experience permanency propels us to ascend in consciousness.

3. CONSCIOUSNESS

Flashes Of Higher Consciousness

Insights, intuitions or epiphanies are like flashes of higher consciousness. Our soul's connection to pure consciousness is continuous and is completed after death. Discernible experience of this connection is a function of the extent of our mental conditions and the lower self or ego. The clearer and purer the mind and heart, the easier is access to lights of the soul within the heart.

Flashes of consciousness can become beams of light upon which the awakened being rides. Spiritual practices and meditations are attempts to connect our normal state of conditioned consciousness to higher consciousness—as beamed from our soul.

> *Higher consciousness is our enduring nature and reality; and the closer we are to it the more we feel secure in its presence.*

Shadows Of Consciousness

Shadows are formed because of light. So too the light of consciousness produces many shadows and darkness. One end of the spectrum of consciousness is complete boundlessness and the other end is dimmed with human veils and limitations—a consciousness black hole.

Human consciousness encompasses body, mind and soul. A pain in a finger focuses the attention to relieve that disorder. This is the shadow that indicates the light; the desire to be stable and safe.

Death is the end of personal conditioned consciousness. Human life is partial consciousness yearning for awakening to permanent and complete consciousness.

There is no light without shadow; consciousness is a light with its own shadows and spectrum – except for supreme consciousness.

3. CONSCIOUSNESS

Living Consciousness

Anything that has a beginning in existence will have an end. The realization of this truth is the cause of much suffering as well as the drive towards awakening to Reality and higher consciousness. The ultimate equalizer and revealer of truth is death. At that point the illusions of past, present and future are revealed. Higher consciousness prevails.

If we do not refer to higher consciousness and the eternal soul within the heart then it is natural that all disconnections and ends such as death will grieve us. Life on earth is like a transfer station leading to another destination—the hereafter. There lies freedom from earthly uncertainties and mental illusions and confusion.

Every awareness and consciousness emerges from a wide and deep field of total consciousness—boundless and eternal.

Types Of Intelligence

Intelligence connects the material and visible world with feelings, emotions and values. Intelligence evolves through nature and nurture and is complex. There have been numerous attempts to measure its values and define it, such as IQ, EQ and SQ.

Intelligence enables us to connect cause and effect, patterns, cycles, and other realities occurring within time and space.

Spiritual intelligence transcends the sensory and physical world beyond mind and intellect. That higher zone of consciousness supersedes all else. This is the home of the human soul and it is what the self aspires toward. The practice of intelligence leads to the lights of the heart—the sacred soul and source of divine inspirations.

> *The wise will climb to the highest mountain to meet the intelligent one, and will desperately avoid the company of an idiot.*

3. CONSCIOUSNESS

Awakened, Illumined & Enlightened

Our quest for knowledge and understanding of life is at two levels: through intelligence and intellect, as well as through a higher zone which is beyond mind and reason—the heart and soul.

An awakened being realizes that mental processes are only outer aspect of consciousness. Higher consciousness is the zone of lights from which invisible and visible entities emerge. When normal mental activity and thoughts cease, you are along the path that leads to the origin of creation.

An enlightened being is constantly aware of supreme consciousness—the source of the universe.

The human journey in life is an ascent in consciousness from what we consider normal, towards the full spectrum—Cosmic Oneness.

Life Is Now

The idea of eternity is a major force in human drives. The present moment – Now – is in itself the beginning of infinity and its agent. The Now connects with the changing times and thus it is timeless. It creates the experience of time.

It is a deep drive in humans to capture the now, to be in the now, to succeed now, and to be happy now. Our obsession to control the present or fix it is due to our subconscious obsession with our soul's eternal nature—a perpetual now.

Most spiritual practices are attempts to go beyond mind and into the infinity of the present now. The perfection of a moment brings about well-beingness and engulfs us – perpetually perfect.

> *The state of constant presence is the nature of our soul, which is the source of our life. Mindfulness draws attention to the present.*

3. CONSCIOUSNESS

Constantly Changeable

Whatever exists has the tendency to continue. Its origin is eternal and is continuous—and it attempts to be perpetual. All creations also tend to connect. Being born into the confines of space-time limitations does not obliterate the original memory of the infinitude of the original singularity and primal gatheredness.

Everything in creation changes, mutates, and carries traces of its earlier state. Whatever changes, also echoes an aspect of its earlier state. It continues to be changeable from constant unchangeability. The flavour of stillness, constancy and continuity show themselves in the tendency to stop change—peace at last as it was in the beginning.

> *All change and variation emanate from the perfect stillness and boundless uniqueness of the One source. All of existence is an emanation of return from The ONE.*

SPECTRUM OF REALITY

Grey, Black & White

There are numerous shades of grey filling the gap between black and white. Most of our experiences are shades of grey. Original light veils its brightness and power by appearing as grey.

You cannot discern darkness or lies unless there is a spark of light or truth. Connectedness is infinite and nothing is ever in isolation in our universe. The mind's tendency is binary as well as analogue; it can connect dualities—good and bad, black and white or grey, alive and dead—as well as endless gradients in between.

All of life's experiences are shades of light and darkness between attraction and repulsion. No pleasure is without pain and no life is without the seed of death. Yet light's essence is without colour and life in essence is boundless.

We experience conditioned consciousness within dualities and opposites—the supreme consciousness is Oneness itself.

3. CONSCIOUSNESS

Quest For Paradise

From ancient times, human beings imagined a state that was beyond pain and pleasure—constant bliss. This idea was given different labels and names, including paradise. Nowadays we travel to that destiny by transcending thoughts, identities and the limitations of space and time. As such, the longing for paradise expresses all of human endeavours and quests. Our soul within our heart carries the paradisiacal model.

Paradise resides in the pure heart and unless it is experienced, there can be no lasting contentment and joy. We love gardens and flowers and we are equally upset when they are damaged or lost. We long for our origin of perfect beingness with no fear, care, need or desire. Utter perfection.

> *Whatever we do points towards a state of perpetual contentment and bliss which is the state of paradise.*

Outer & Inner Awareness

There are always at least two viewpoints at any time. You can face the past or the future, origin or destination. You observe and hear what is outside of you or reflect upon your inner senses and feelings. You are always held in between these two zones and desire balance and stability. This tension enables us to grow and evolve physically, mentally and spiritually.

Everything that exists has an outer and an inner facet, which are in balance. For a youngster, most experiences are due to sensory stimulation. For an adult there is outer and inner consciousness. For an awakened being the outer and inner are seamlessly bound together due to the emergence of the light of the Oneness.

> *Discriminating between outer and inner is the first step to realizing their inseparability in essence.*

3. CONSCIOUSNESS

Asset & Liability Of Memory

Experience is the result of connections between an inner sense and an outer event. Memory is the child of this union and is born in the neurons' nursing home from where it can be recalled. With repeated activation, a memory becomes established and even emerges unconsciously. Nature and nurture facilitate the connection between stimulation and response that produces a depository of personal recollection within the mind.

Memory is a great asset when it relates to survival and well-beingness. Emotionally and psychologically, painful or negative memories can be harmful, and manifest as a disorder that may require special attention. Spiritual progress occurs by transcending all memory to the higher soul consciousness, beyond asset or liability.

> *For day-to-day functioning, a healthy memory is a great asset. For transformation and awakening to Reality, mind, senses and identity are a barrier.*

Root Of Exaggeration

Whatever we experience has an impact on our mind and leaves traces in us. Self-expression is important for human evolvement and growth and this need can become exaggerated in order to be noticed.

A child who wants to attract attention to a discovery or achievement may shout or exaggerate what may be to others insignificant. One's own personal experience is important; we are naturally self-centred. What pains you is important beyond what others think about it. There is a natural tendency for the self to exaggerate. The soul is in utter ease and contentment. The self needs to shout to exert itself. The shadow of the Real wants to assert itself.

> *Whatever concerns you at body, mind and heart level is given great importance and prominence; we are creatures given to exaggeration.*

3. CONSCIOUSNESS

Suffering & Liberation

Good thoughts, good speech and good actions have been regarded as a universal code of desirable conduct. The best of actions emanate from a clear mind and a loving heart.

Suffering is a human condition due to conflicting forces affecting head and heart. The demands and desires of the senses and the mind are endless. We suffer due to mental distraction, confusions and inappropriate actions. Suffering can be a positive force towards awakening when its nature and origin are discovered.

Liberation is transcending the animal self within us. This self is important for early growth and survival, but becomes a handicap and obstacle for spiritual unfoldment and awakening to the light of the soul.

> *For a child the ego is the friend; for a mature person it is the enemy. Liberation is to transcend the lower self and live as a soul.*

SPECTRUM OF REALITY

Competition To Cooperation

Competition is due to proximity of two or more related entities or forces. It is plurality seeking unity: the quest of original Oneness. With less fear of survival and ego, the power of cooperation, friendship and collective goodness can prevail. Short-term self-interest yields to higher interest and greater goodness. These moves are towards higher consciousness.

At the base animal level, there is always some competition as well as cooperation—the main concern being survival and continuity. At the higher levels of human consciousness, cooperation and love may reduce the illusion of separation and otherness. Beams of Oneness illumine the path towards its reality of Oneness.

The light of the original Oneness can turn harsh competition to flowing and easy cooperation.

3. CONSCIOUSNESS

Dreams

From ancient times the idea of what is real and what is not has challenged human thought. There are different zones of consciousness, as there are different realities. During our wakeful state, we consider most sharable experiences as real, but what is real about a dream?

A healthy working relationship between our senses, mind and heart develop to reconcile the ever-changing evolving self and the constant soul. We link physics and metaphysics, our sensory reality and Reality.

Dreams and sleep are essential for human health—to reorder, fit and connect day-to-day experiences and past memory, and enable our temporary life to be nourished by the soul's light.

The enlightened being regards all normal experiences as a dream. Common dreams are merely dreams within a dream.

4. Connectedness

SPECTRUM OF CONNECTEDNESS

- ✠ Rooted In Oneness
- ✠ Illusion Of Separation
- ✠ Levels Of Connectedness
- ✠ Purpose Of Connectedness
- ✠ Connected By Love
- ✠ Body, Mind & Heart
- ✠ Causes, Effects & Correlations
- ✠ The Particle & Its Wave
- ✠ Obscured By Light & Darkness
- ✠ Exclusivity, Inclusivity & Singularity
- ✠ Relationships With Others
- ✠ Belonging
- ✠ Language Connects & Repels
- ✠ Bonded By Joy Or Adversity
- ✠ Disconnection Through Suicide
- ✠ Thrill Of Rare Connections

SPECTRUM OF REALITY

- ✠ Curse And Virtue Of Familiarity
- ✠ Punishment By Disconnection
- ✠ Connection With A Master

Introduction

Everything that exists reveals aspects of its state, condition and direction. All earthly and material realities are interconnected with relevant energy fields. Visible light is a minute fraction of the enormous electromagnetic field. The numerous levels of interconnectedness between matter and energy are like the fabric or foundation of consciousness.

In the visible world what connects is the outer evidence of much deeper unseen connections. From the flash of the big bang, space and time exploded into universal dimensions. Cosmic rays and numerous fields of energies penetrate the entire universal realities along patterns and designs that can be discerned most of the time.

Countless forces demonstrate connectedness at numerous levels of physical, chemical, and electrical levels and other invisible levels— all had emerged from a singularity and spread out into countless pluralities.

Original Oneness and connectedness is traceable in all human intentions and action. We love to be at one with what we desire. Proximity, gatheredness and other bonds play their part for us to experience connectedness—at body, mind and heart levels. We are alive due to our connection with the soul within the heart—transmitting its energies and life force drawn from the cosmic soul.

Discerning connectedness reduces the illusion of sensory distance and separation from source. It is the bridge between conditioned consciousness and cosmic Reality—that which is self-sustaining and integrated in itself.

Rooted In Oneness

Intelligence, knowledge, ability and desires are all different channels that lead to the natural human drive to know, understand and relate to connections. Love, imagination and creativity enhance connectedness and union. We always strive to reduce distance and separation. The rapid speed of travel and communication are attempts to shrink space back to original Oneness.

The human soul beams consciousness based on universal connectedness. The normal consciousness that experiences distance and separation is the driving force to experience the cosmic nature of the soul.

We long to belong. Imprisonment, segregation and separation are resented and are regarded as rejection and distance. The self belongs to its soul, which also belongs to the sacred spirit.

> *Our life is totally entangled with the sacred cosmic oneness. All our earthly quests aim to experience this Reality.*

4. CONNECTEDNESS

Illusion Of Separation

The mother holds the newborn tight to reduce the shock of separation. We love union and gatheredness.

Illusions give indications of Reality. If it were not for pain we would not cherish its absence, and if it were not for loss, we would not be questing gain. Human drives are aimed towards higher consciousness, which reveals universal connectedness and ongoingness. Our ego self and soul or spirit, are inseparable until death—then a new pattern of connection begins.

The mind helps us to experience connectedness at the sensory level, intellect, and at subtler levels of the heart. What we always crave is the bliss of contentment, and security in experiencing cosmic Oneness—no separation or distance: to be at one with eternal Reality.

> *The illusion of separation is a driving force toward the conclusion—Universal Oneness, perpetual singularity.*

Levels Of Connectedness

The universe is interconnected at countless levels from the most minute to the galactic. It is the extent of discernibility of these connections and forces that is sought by us.

The newly born baby connects with its mother. After a few weeks emotions develop; eye contact and feelings bring about deeper connections. With maturity, subtler senses, feelings and connections develop.

Consciousness of connections originates from our soul within the heart and takes physical, chemical, intellectual and other dimensions. From that origin, numerous forces of connectedness emerge, most of which are invisible.

> *The different levels of connectedness and their priorities are understood due to the mind which is illumined by the soul.*

4. CONNECTEDNESS

Purpose Of Connectedness

Our search for ancestral origins is often accompanied by the hope that a famous ancestor may emerge. Humans like to be associated with fame and fortune. The self yearns to be important, special, and associate with merit and power.

The origin of the force that drives us to experience connectedness emanates from our soul, which is entangled with the cosmic soul. The human self-ego craves desirable earthly connections associated with knowledge, wealth and other qualities; these are latent beams constantly radiating from our soul. When we transcend conditioned consciousness, we realize the end of separation and feelings of disconnectedness. What we desire is to awaken to the source of life and the origin of consciousness and life.

Whatever we think or do, we seek aspects of connectedness; A drive towards Oneness.

Connected By Love

Love is a field of energy that brings close, connects and unites what is under its power. Love's field has a wide range of strands and zones of intensity and durability.

Some connections occur quickly and fall apart quickly. Others begin slowly and become durable, and others happen all of a sudden and then evolve. Like a fire, when love is nurtured it may grow and blossom; when neglected it may dissipate and die.

Love between two people may start with shared interests or physical, mental or other attraction. When the heart has opened to love, passion and obsession may follow. Lovers can taste aspects of Oneness when the hearts are in unison at the gateway of Oneness — the fountainhead of love.

All aspects of love emanate from the original divine love that connects and links the entire universe.

4. CONNECTEDNESS

Body, Mind & Heart

Our senses, body and mind are our first steps of discovery and experience. Memory connects past to present. The mind then projects toward the future. We soon learn the importance of clear thoughts and a disciplined mind.

Those who seek higher levels of consciousness practice meditation, religious and spiritual disciplines to transcend mental states and sensory experiences to pure consciousness. A healthy body, a clear mind and pure heart are preconditions of experiencing a wholesome balance of our material and spiritual composition. Mind connects the soul with the material world and heart is the doorway to the soul and eternal spirit.

> *A healthy enhanced connection between body, mind and heart is necessary for progress towards higher consciousness.*

Causes, Effects & Correlations

The entire universe resonates and vibrates in interactive ways. There are infinite varieties of stimulation and response, transmission and reception, and numerous reflections, refractions and deflections. The mind looks for connection between cause and effect. Much of science is decoding cause and effect relationships.

We are obsessed with understanding connections, especially subtler and invisible relationships. In our normal world cause and effect are easier to discern than the realms of the very small or the very big.

Sometimes several events happen together but coincidences and correlations may simply accompany cause and effect. In complex situations, we can mistake coincidences or correlations as causes.

Human life is based upon connections with different threads of life—the original cause is ONE and the universe is the effect.

4. CONNECTEDNESS

The Particle & Its Wave

An active mind is like a hunting dog looking for its prey. Its main task is to connect and continue and therefore it seeks preservation and ongoingness – habits and timelessness. The senses, mind, emotions and memory all conspire to create a personal image and identity. It is how a photon becomes a particle and appears to disconnect from its wave origin.

The photon is both a particle as well as a wave function. So is the human composition. The particle is the equivalent of the self, or ego; and the wave is the soul or spirit. The mind often reinforces the ego and identity; only when transcended is the souls light experienced. The more we resonate with our own soul, the higher the state of our consciousness and contentment.

> *Self-identity and concern is an early stage of evolvement towards the discovery of the universal soul. The particle now yields to its wave origin and is in unity.*

SPECTRUM OF REALITY

Obscured By Light & Darkness

The light and heat of the sun was modified, filtered and reduced over millions of years before life on earth could begin.

During the day, the light of the sun obscures the millions of galaxies that are visible at night. On a pitch-dark night, we cannot see anything. Light is necessary to discern profiles in the dark. Extreme light and total darkness disconnect us from seeing what is already there.

Our sensory experiences are indicators for our spiritual journey; the path can be obscured by the extent of light or darkness. Ego-self darkness blocks the light and absolute divine light is so immense. That remains in its singularity.

> *We are creatures between dense darkness and cosmic light. Our median position gives us the advantage of witnessing Reality in its fullness.*

4. CONNECTEDNESS

Exclusivity, Inclusivity & Singularity

The universe is effulgence from singularity and each of us is a microcosm carrying traces of the macrocosm. Respect for other beings, love, and honour for life affirms sanctity of the human soul. Everyone has the potential to realize the grace of having an exclusive sacred soul.

To be unjust towards others is to be unjust towards one's own soul, as all souls are the same. Most humans consider themselves to be special and resent being deprived of anything good or pleasant.

The soul knows its universal origin and the divine qualities embedded in it. Demeaning others is demeaning a soul, excluding others is excluding yourself, and that is unjust and disturbing of life's natural flow.

The human soul carries the imprints of God. The self strives towards that state and its qualities and shuns rejection and prejudices.

SPECTRUM OF REALITY

Relationships With Others

Friends connect, share and communicate at several levels. Lovers connect and resonate often beyond words and sounds. Those close in mind and heart relate beyond words and action. As for those who are in the ocean of Oneness there is only rejoicing that transcends any description – they are at one.

From early awareness, human life is an exercise to relate, connect and unite, as well as to reject and avoid what is incompatible. Our outer relationships involve the physical, mental and other forces, much of which are not obvious, especially the soul. Connections at higher level of consciousness are more durable.

When the self is at unison with the soul, all relationships fit in with ease and harmony.

The subtler the main attractive force in a relationship, the more durable it is. Realising Oneness is the most powerful force.

4. CONNECTEDNESS

Belonging

It is painful when one is rejected and does not belong to a larger group. It is a deprivation for a grown up and a tragedy for the young.

Physically we connect and belong. Culturally we look for like-minded people to share habits and expected behaviour.

Belonging is in two zones, one is at the human level of conditioned consciousness and the other at the heart and soul zone. There are patterns of attraction that relate and connect these two zones. Contentment in the heart zone and the spiritual level makes the human sphere of secondary importance. The reverse is not true. All belongs to the One and we quest this state.

> *In sacred presence belonging is a redundant word: there is only the light from which everything emanates and to which all returns.*

Language Connects & Repels

Everything in existence discloses its characteristics in multiple ways. Beautiful crystals vibrate and reveal their chemical and physical nature. All living entities declare aspects of their qualities as dominant reality. These signals, languages and transmissions are countless and occur at numerous levels.

Communication between two people can enhance the quality of their humanity as well as spirituality. Faulty communication can also diminish the quality of connection. Language can bring about goodness and hope, or increase darkness and despair. The beautiful language of the soul is modified by the time it reaches mind and body. The sacred language of Oneness is the origin of all that we hear and know—it brings about human liberation and sustainable contentment. All else are dilutions or diversions. The primal language only declares Oneness.

Language can enhance well-beingness or diminish and darken life.

4. CONNECTEDNESS

Bonded By Joy Or Adversity

At the level of basic survival, the memory becomes sharp. Recollecting good times, happiness, and sharing these states with others reinforces bonds and special connections.

When facing danger, or in fear for life, we touch the root of connectedness. During wars, consciousness is focused upon survival and at that level, the memory becomes vivid and deep. Warriors' celebrations are deeply emotional.

Special anniversaries leave a mark on the human psyche. Attendees of special sports events, games or festivals, remember the state where thousands of people connected in one cheer or loud acknowledgement. Any occasion that brings the collective consciousness to single pointedness becomes memorable—we all merged from Oneness.

The beginning of existence and its end is Oneness and in-between we take delight in the experiences of deep connectedness.

Disconnection Through Suicide

The natural human drive is to evolve from total concern with body, mind and senses towards higher and subtler states of consciousness. Our drive to explore and expand consciousness is to deepen connections between the seen and the unseen. When we remain exclusively within conditioned consciousness, life can appear as dull and meaningless. The extreme case is suicide, that is, to end what is unacceptable—a dead end.

Much of human dysfunctionality, depression and psychological disorders are due to the dim connection with heart, the soul and inner perfections. When life's purpose of being in unison with the soul is neglected, then spiritual nourishment diminishes and despair and suicide tendencies may set in. The lower self and ego create the black hole and suicide.

> *Physical suicide is a material expression of spiritual darkness and lack of resonance with the soul.*

4. CONNECTEDNESS

Thrill Of Rare Connections

The whole universe is interconnected and we experience separation and distance as veils on original Oneness.

Insights increase with imagination, meditation and transcendence beyond mind and time. Touching the infinite zone of our spirit is a rare and most delightful experience.

Generally we explore what is tangible but to experience the lights of the soul requires an inner technology that stops all mental activity and lets one drift into a higher zone of consciousness.

We value rare gemstones or artefacts. The rarest of all entities is the soul within our heart and to realize this gift requires giving up all other sights. We need to transcend our so-called real world to the Real, rare world — the dominant unseen.

Our relentless drive to know what is considered important may take us to the source of life itself—the precious soul.

Curse And Virtue Of Familiarity

By nature a human being is investigative and curious; we are always looking for the new and rare. Whatever is familiar is often overlooked or ignored. The soul's presence is taken for granted and therefore its light is veiled by mental habits, thoughts and identity; thus it is not clearly recognised, yet it is present and is the source of life.

What is familiar does not attract attention. We seek new stimulations and avoid what is common or boring. The self or ego enjoys the familiar and what it is habitually used to. That is how identity is developed. This state is a hindrance to spiritual progress. We need a balance between familiar humanity and the challenge of spirituality. Our life's purpose is to experience and know the sacred soul within the heart.

Discovery of truth requires transcendence of the familiar and access to the subtle and unseen—the ever present soul.

4. CONNECTEDNESS

Punishment By Disconnection

A mother's disapproval of a child contains the threat of censure, disconnection or rejection. Society also disapproves and ostracizes by punishing with imprisonment or isolation. Disconnection is a threat to life.

We seek wider and deeper connectedness in different zones of existence. Failure often implies a disconnection or missing an aspect of connection. In business, forecasting and predictions imply connecting with the upsurge or the down surge of a market.

We seek approval, acceptance and connectedness at physical, mental, emotional and spiritual levels. The soul is ever connected to the cosmic essence.

The universe is ever connected and the life force is ever continuous. Any disconnection is a deprivation.

Connection With A Master

When you are in the proximity of an illumined being and benefit from his or her state, your life's direction may change. The company we keep always affects us. You may return to your old habits when away from the influence of the awakened being. Harmony is proximity to peace, ease, and origin, and the use of a tuning fork is to recalibrate that harmony. An effective master or role model is like a tuning fork.

Followers of teachers and spiritual masters are at risk of assuming the continuity of the inner state they had experienced due to the presence of an illumined being. We need proximity of the light of a master, until the soul within the heart becomes the master and authority. When one's candle is fully lit, then the inner light leads.

Proximity to the light of a master and commitment to the path is a necessary step to inner illumination and enlightenment.

5. Continuity

SPECTRUM OF CONTINUITY

- ✠ Consciousness Of Time
- ✠ The Past's Future
- ✠ Past, Present & Future
- ✠ Perpetual Reality
- ✠ Now Is Eternal
- ✠ Temporal & Eternal Life
- ✠ Death: Friend Or Foe?
- ✠ Celebrating The Soul
- ✠ Respecting The Departed
- ✠ Quest For Longevity
- ✠ How Old Are You Really?
- ✠ Seductive Habits
- ✠ Hindsight, Insight & Foresight
- ✠ Imprint Of Past Generations
- ✠ Lineage & Ancestry
- ✠ A Desirable Legacy
- ✠ History As A Thread Of Continuity

SPECTRUM OF REALITY

- ✠ Dynasties
- ✠ Eternal Love

Introduction

What was there before the beginning of creation? The beginning implies movement and change within space and time. The start of the universe is what is popularly referred to as the big bang. Most human endeavours occur along the path of increasing consciousness and awareness, growing knowledge of wider and deeper connections, and more profound relationships in existence.

We try to move faster than time, or stop and freeze time. The fear of death and the desirability of experiencing eternity now are major forces in the human quest. If we stop all thoughts and self-awareness, we may be at the door of the eternal moment – at the beginning of it all! Beginnings and end are merged together.

Once the taste buds of experiencing timelessness are awakened, with spiritual evolvement we may come to realize the presence of eternity within our own heart: the perpetual now – a consciousness that is beyond time and space.

Our aims for longevity, stability, power, ability and other desirable attributes have their source in our own heart, for these are qualities radiating from the soul. Foreverness is the divine nature, and our soul reflects that. We desire continuity for what is considered attractive and helpful in our well-beingness and this limited attempt at continuity is a prelude to the energy field of perpetual presence and timelessness. Our mind cannot realize this extraordinary state because it works within the framework of space and time. Continuity is the source, which encompasses our humanity and divinity. Continuity is the nature of our own soul. It is our essential nature.

SPECTRUM OF REALITY

5. CONTINUITY

Consciousness Of Time

Having our roots in the infinitude of timelessness the human experience of distance and movement is a constant challenge.

To transcend time you need to follow a trustworthy map and live along a path that unifies shadows and lights. Self and soul will merge in unison and then we accept the constraints of time, whilst the souls light remind us of eternity.

Time exists in the zone of our limitations and earthiness. When time stops all separations end and what remains is pure boundless consciousness. This is the nature of our soul.

Human consciousness is limited but the quest for higher consciousness beyond space and time is constant.

SPECTRUM OF REALITY

The Past's Future

Past and future are illusory mental experiences whose reality will be revealed by death. All events are a mere interplay between energy and forms with an attached meaning, which leave a trace as memory.

The past has no independent or sustainable existence; the future is the same. As for the present, the moment contains all: a magisterial treasure.

When the heart is pure then the light of the Soul illumines all. The 'present' carries some memory of the past but the intensity of the present moment echoes eternity: a now that permeates all and gives rise to the experience of time that drives us towards the timeless Now.

The present gives rise to all that is perceived within space and time—that is sacred presence! The perfect now.

5. CONTINUITY

Past, Present & Future

Everything that exists is subject to change and is not self-sustaining. Past and future are temporary traces connected through mind and memory. All events are a mere interplay between energy, form, and meaning which leave some traces in existence. As for the present, that is the mystery. It contains all, yet there is No Thing in the present—it is in time, yet free of time.

The present contains all that is perceivable within space and time, i.e. our universe. That sacred presence is the reality of the soul or spirit within the heart. Happiness is according to the quality of well-beingness of the heart. When the heart is pure then the light of the soul illumines the being with the intense reality of the present moment.

> *Now is not caught within space or time, but simply gives rise to illusions of time. Now represents eternal presence appearing in time.*

Perpetual Reality

A mature mind can recognize what is transient and changeable and what is more durable. We enjoy the changing seasons and excitement of uncertainty, but our main quest is for what is reliable and constant. A relationship that connects human excitement and stimulation with spiritual stability and tranquillity is a durable relationship.

There are endless levels of realities and the higher points are near the origin of what is constant and perpetual. Whatever reminds us of the ever-present is generally a desirable state. The ever-changing ego celebrates its perpetual origin, the soul within the heart, with remembrance of birthdays or other reminders of the Real.

The soul is a reflector of what is eternal and perpetual and enables us to appreciate an experience of eternal Reality.

5. CONTINUITY

Now Is Eternal

Identity relates to mind, memory and time. Thoughts connect the past to the present and future. Reflection, meditation and the silent mind enable us to experience the immense present moment— now.

Much human effort is expended to reduce distance and separation. As for time, we try to go faster than all possibilities or, more effectively, to stop time altogether. Our human conditioned consciousness drives us towards stillness in mind, which opens the door of timelessness and perpetual presence. All human endeavours lead to a point of experience, which occurs when the mind is content and still. The moment of success or heightened pleasure reflects this state. Within the still moment lies the zone of transcendence of mind and time. That is the infinitude of Reality.

When the past is lost and the future is of no concern, the perfection of now is a great gift that yields a lasting thrill.

Temporal & Eternal Life

The experience of separation and movement of time are the natural human limitations that we need to sublimate. Our earthly life is part-time, short and restricted, yet we are obsessed with eternal life and boundlessness. This drive often appears as the elusive grasp of longevity or love of immortality.

What makes death easy, natural and acceptable is the personal experience of cosmic consciousness and boundless life. When this reality is understood and lived, earthly death will be regarded as a natural part of spiritual evolution and the perfection of the cycle of return to origin; matter back to earth and soul to heavens.

We love life and consciousness in every way it appears. We love the permanent, the source of creation—the soul within us radiates that state.

5. CONTINUITY

Death: Friend Or Foe?

Fear is a natural human drive rooted in the need for earthly survival. Fear, hope and other emotions are natural drives that can lead to soul consciousness and spiritual awakening by transcending mind and identification with body and the cycle of its birth and death.

With higher consciousness, the soul will override the mind and death becomes a natural outcome of temporary life. The enlightened person knows that death is simply a demarcation of moving from the transitory experience of earth to the ongoingness of life hereafter. The physical side of our composition returns to the pool of earthly matter and the soul reverts to the cosmic ocean of lights.

> *Fear of death is a natural state of the human condition that can lead to the realisation of the ever-living soul. The sage regards death as a loyal friend who reminds one of the earthly transition.*

Celebrating The Soul

Commemorations are often tinged with some nostalgia or melancholy. Celebrating the birth of a person who had influenced and helped others, especially during afflictions, is to remember a desirable connection and its continuation.

There is no pleasure without displeasure, no hope without fear. Yet our tendency is to remember hope and success more than despair or failure. We reinforce good memories with photos or objects that bestow deeper reality to the event. The soul is in utter perfection and that is what the enlightened person celebrates continuously. That is true worship.

It is human nature to be optimistic and to expect better times in the future. Our spiritual nature propels us to experience the perfection of the present moment.

5. CONTINUITY

Respecting The Departed

Marriage, birth, along with traditions regarding death and burial, tell us much about the spiritual state of cultures. Our life is bounded by earthly arrival and departure. In between we try to gain understanding, knowledge and clarity of meaning and direction.

Generally people highlight the good deeds of the deceased. We like to honour the dead even if their faults outweighed their virtues. The subconscious feeling regarding the soul and its mystery even bestows greater respect upon a person after death. Respect for cemeteries and reprehension for desecration of the dead reflect special consideration for departed human souls as well as for the body which was its temporary home.

Goodness becomes clearer after its loss. Respect for the dead is due to the sacredness of the soul which has now left its body where it belongs.

Quest For Longevity

Older people are often nostalgic about youthfulness and work hard to maintain good health and well-beingness. Our physical and mental capacities have considerable limitations, but not our spiritual reality. The soul is boundless in its perfection and its light transmits life to us.

Spiritual light overrides all other shadows as the soul illuminates fears and concerns about aging and death. The urgency and desire for longevity is understandable for a person who has not experienced the soul's blissful state. The quest to prolong human life on earth is justifiable to gain this experience otherwise it is foolish and futile. Whatever we quest for in our lifetime is a reflection of what already resides within our own soul—the ever-living, perfect light.

> *Human life is a short bridge that leads to the experience of the eternal nature of one's own soul.*

5. CONTINUITY

How Old Are You Really?

Children often like to be thought of as older in age. They enjoy birthdays and 'growing up'. Most old people prefer to preserve some youthfulness and are apprehensive about old age and death. For an old person, continuity of life and fear of death are big issues.

A few fortunate people are able to transcend the limitations of identity and mind to the timeless zone of the soul. The soul is like a holographic representation of eternity.

So how old are you really? Indeed, who are you? Do you rely upon your biographical script and memory or upon the spiritual light within your heart? When you know who you really are, you lose concern about years.

Age and years denote earth's turning around the sun. Humans are celestial beings experiencing an earthly journey.

Seductive Habits

When a specific aspect of consciousness or experience repeats itself, it becomes habitual. This repetition brings about a reassuring feeling of connectedness and continuation. Habits have a seductive aspect of hinting at ongoingness, continuity and perpetuity.

Habits enhance identity and material productivity. Breaking habits is a drive to experience new horizons along the direction that may lead to higher horizons of consciousness.

Regular meditation to transcend the limitations of the mind is a good habit that helps us out of the illusive habits of the lower self towards consciousness and awakening to the Real.

Mind and body prefer repetitiveness and familiarity— false security. Spirituality requires breaking norms and experiencing the lights of the soul.

5. CONTINUITY

Hindsight, Insight & Foresight

Our mental capacity and senses are limited and give only an approximation of facts and events. That is why differentiations between good and bad are constantly changing and cause confusion. What may be disliked today can be celebrated tomorrow.

Higher consciousness reveals perfection in all levels of existence. Spiritual insight connects the short-lived personal life to its original sacredness. With higher consciousness, you see order within chaos and mercy in disasters. You see death as a natural relief and birth as a challenge and potential affliction.

Human beings are often described as the middle people — between physics and metaphysics, heavenly and earthly, this life and the hereafter. Our challenge is to connect sight with insight and be on earth with access to higher consciousness and soul reference.

> *The senses connect the visible with its meaning. With hindsight, foresight improves. Truth is the primal light that transcends senses and mind.*

SPECTRUM OF REALITY

Imprint Of Past Generations

The present moment is a result of the past, and the future is the outcome of the past and present — an ongoing thread of our intentions and the directions we take. From the beginning of creation, every new event carries the traces of its past and the hints of its future.

Memories of origin and the past are carried over until the end. We can trace influences of our ancestors for many generations in the past. When man started to domesticate animals, the importance of blood and genes were realised. From medieval times, concern about 'bad blood' implied some deficiencies. Some of our latent tendencies may have come from past generations. The original light within us is the most dominant force in life and can overcome epigenetic handicaps.

Connection and continuation are dominant in human consciousness —at all stages of life and existence.

5. CONTINUITY

Lineage & Ancestry

The awakened being is not concerned with biological lineage. Childhood events and the past are remembered as a distant haze. Spiritual amnesia spares him much of the drama of what is called normal life and remembrance and difficult past and experiences.

The human soul is of heavenly origin and is already 'noble'; thus arises the human subconscious notion of being of extraordinary ancestry. Once you know your soul, then the idea or search for a noble origin fades away. Your present spiritual potential and reality is greater than imaginable. On occasions you may think you are superior and better than the 'other' is, or you may even feel that one day your greatness will be discovered – these feelings are due to a flash of light from your 'heavenly' soul. The lower self also shows our earthly animal side—what an intricate balance!

Enlightenment implies transcendence from basic human consciousness — when you experience the sacredness of your soul's origin—the cosmic soul.

A Desirable Legacy

The innate force to continue and procreate has accompanied life on earth. Diverse creations continued to reveal the intensity of the force of ongoingness and duplication.

It is a natural desire to foresee the future and leave behind what will be regarded as good and helpful for higher consciousness, connection and continuation. The hope for good roots and legacy moves onto the future for a better and happier situation for human beings—better balanced as earthly creatures with heavenly roots.

The soul's lineage and destiny is the original Oneness. The self and limited human consciousness, replicate this reality along earthly lights and shadows.

> *Human consciousness strives to experience the soul's state—perfecting presence points towards the quest of a better future destiny.*

5. CONTINUITY

History As A Thread Of Continuity

What we learn from history or the past is a perennial topic of debate; we draw from it ideas and lessons to give legitimacy to our own values.

Past, personal and collective history is a mixture of events, myths, facts and views, opinions and values linked to those occurrences. History is reviewed and re-evaluated regularly. Memory is often renewed and updated. Since everything in life is relative and changeable, what help can we really gain from the past?

An awakened individual reads history as the ascent of human consciousness towards its origin. Each human being is challenged to be liberated from the cycle of action and stillness. A few live as heavenly spirits – maybe a few more attempt to awaken to the truth of the soul.

> *The enlightened view of history and the desire to study and learn from it indicates the power and force of continuity and its echo of timelessness.*

Dynasties

From early settlements in ancient times, the issue of dynasty and inheritance of power or wealth were of great importance. Close family marriage and even incest was practised in order to preserve dynastic power. During the past centuries, many kings and rulers tried to create a dynasty that carries their names and deeds into the future. Most failed. There is no permanency in the temporary realm. What is permanent is God's light, beyond space and time.

For many people, lineage or name provides status and the illusion of immortality. Present day corporations try to be independent of human life and can often live much longer than any of their employees. Enlightened beings know that personal experience of life is only a means to awaken to eternal life—hence there is no need for dynastic continuation. The soul continues.

Our love for continuation manifests in numerous ways, like leaving behind a legacy or progeny. Only the Real continues and all human endeavours carry traces of the real.

5. CONTINUITY

Eternal Love

Love is the universal agent of eternal Oneness. Love brings about connection, closeness and a measure of fusion and unity between diverse entities.

Human intentions, actions and attention ultimately point toward Oneness and unity. The reverse or shadow of this drive is also close by. Enmity is the dark side of friendship as hate is to love. These dualities are born together and die together. When these values, ideas and thoughts are transcended, then the power of original love eliminates dualities revealing cosmic sacred unity. God's boundlessness gives rise to limited earthly consciousness and human love—a prelude to being at one with eternal Love.

Similarities in mind and emotions are preludes to experiencing aspects of sameness and oneness—where eternal love ends all differences and separation.

6. Human Beings

SPECTRUM OF HUMAN BEING

- Body, Mind & Soul
- Separation & Identity
- Love Of Self And Soul Realization
- Hierarchy Of The Human Quest
- Emotions & Feelings
- Nature & Nurture
- Paradoxes & Contradictions
- Change & Constancy
- Duty & Responsibility
- Love & Hate
- Levels Of Dependency
- Certainty & Higher Consciousness
- Born Amongst Others
- Others' Faults
- Stability & Prosperity
- Loyalty, Honesty & Reliability
- Creativity & Arts
- Fairness & Sympathy
- Free Will & Determinism

SPECTRUM OF REALITY

- ✠ Pain, Pleasure & Lasting Joy
- ✠ Denials, Deception, Concealment & Lies
- ✠ Weeping & Laughing
- ✠ Sobriety & Intoxication
- ✠ Deception & Lies
- ✠ Sadness & Gladness
- ✠ Empathy & Envy
- ✠ Shyness, Guilt & Shame
- ✠ Generosity & Kindness
- ✠ Mine Or Not Mine?
- ✠ Needs, Thoughts & Actions
- ✠ To Find & Lose
- ✠ Curse & Blessing Of Ego

Introduction

Several cultures and religions have described dramatic myths and metaphors regarding the creation of Adam in paradise. We may correlate the rise of human consciousness with the development of the frontal lobe in early hominids.

Self-awareness, complex communication and consciousness of time and space, as well as past and future, are all part of the evolutionary saga of humankind. At the time of agricultural settlement, a few thousand years ago, our imaginal intelligence soared to levels unknown before. Several groups of hunter/gatherers also tackled the idea of unity as the source of multiplicity and diversity. The idea of God developed into religions and the early foundation of ideas that relate to morality, immorality and conduct.

From early times, the nature of human beings extended across a wide range of consciousness enveloping body, mind, heart and soul. Humanity straddles physical and material realities, connected through spirit and soul. The human soul transmits the web of desirable attributes and qualities through the mind to produce desires, activities and destiny.

Every one of us is challenged to balance the animal inside us with the sacred light of our soul. Everyone is conscious of the quest to connect and to continue at numerous levels, from physics to metaphysics. We seek stability and constancy in a zone whose nature is dynamic and changing. In truth, what we are seeking is our soul, which is like the inner deity and personal God. Every one of us expresses their reality according to genetic memories, connectedness and the play of nature and nurture. We express the ever-changing self until we realize the presence of the constant soul. We experience a brief biography given to us by our spiritual Reality. A human being is a limited entity attempting to express an infinite Reality—human's real nature.

6. HUMAN BEINGS

Body, Mind & Soul

The human soul or spirit is a celestial entity and needs mind and intellect to relate to earthly pluralities and cycles of change. There are many levels of reduction of intensity of power between the divine light and us. The sun's light and radiation had to be reduced considerably before life could begin on earth.

The mind relates and connects with earthly realities whilst illumined by the soul. Human nature is based on matter and energy, but yearns for the light of the soul. When identities are removed and the heart is pure, then the light of the soul shines brightly and leads toward the completion of the journey's purpose. At that point all judgement, contradictions and uncertainties vanish. The divine and eternal nature of the soul becomes effulgent and dominant—God's purpose.

The purpose of human life is complete when total harmony between body, mind and heart is attained and experienced.

Separation & Identity

A human being is composed of both energy and matter. Our physical part contains all the elements on earth and our energy part resonates with astral energies, cosmic rays and countless other invisible forces.

A baby senses its separation early on in life and begins to develop its own identity and individuality. We behave like a laser electron, which becomes a particle when caught in human eyesight. Otherwise, it is an inseparable part of the wave entity. The baby thrives on interactions and stimulation by the mother and others. The ego grows by reflections and acknowledgement. The experience of being separate from others leads to identity, personality and ego. With maturity and wisdom a few may realise that the ego identity was a necessary filter between the soul and its earthly connection. The experience of separation hides our cosmic unity.

Separation and temporary identity (mind, memory and biography) are preludes to the discovery of the Reality of our soul.

6. HUMAN BEINGS

Love Of Self And Soul Realization

Love is the universal connector that radiates from Oneness. The mother's love for the baby stimulates the baby's love for its pets, toys and itself. In childhood, self-love spills over to the love of others and eventually to love of soul.

Love to explore and discover helps with growth and maturity. Then comes love of power, beauty and harmony. Love evolves from material objects to their meanings and intrinsic value.

Unconditional love beams from the soul and illuminates intentions and actions. When the self realises its real origin — the soul within the heart — then Higher Consciousness reveals the sacred True Reality within: Oneness that permeates the universe through the power of love.

When self-love yields to the perfect soul within, then it is at one with the life force that pervades the universe.

Hierarchy Of The Human Quest

Individually and collectively we hope for a better life in the future. Every form has a meaning, a direction and a purpose. Human consciousness spans the sensory, mental and transcendental. A child lives mostly through the sensory, an adult combines the material and mental, and those on a spiritual quest seek to transcend the physical and mental states to higher consciousness.

There is a natural drive towards the transcendental and liberation from all limitation. That state can be experienced when love of oblivion and a no-thought state is practised regularly. The ultimate quest is to live as a soul without denial of its temporary earthly entanglement.

All desires and quests end at the door of higher consciousness, at the point of the soul's perfection.

6. HUMAN BEINGS

Emotions & Feelings

The human brain is perhaps the most complex entity in the universe. The human mind is the miracle that connects the universe with tangible earth. Our mind is the seat of our feelings, which, once internalized, become emotions, and affect our body and life – entangled connectedness.

The soul is the source of power and life that enables the mind to expand in its consciousness, to connect or disconnect, and to continue or stop. Feelings are what we sense due to events and the illusion of values we attach to them. Emotions are the result of feelings that impinge upon us and affect our body, mind, heart and behaviour. All these dynamics are due to the mental connection to the source – the soul.

When emotions and feelings are balanced by intellect, reason and wisdom, then their negative effect is minimal.

Nature & Nurture

Today nature is quite manipulated and controlled by human designs and activities. Nurture is also very different compared to a few decades ago. Our children are subjected to intense specialization and outer education devoid of inner 'technology', health and mental stillness.

We need wholesome bodies, clear minds and pure hearts so that we can experience the full spectrum of life. We need to understand how our bodies, minds and emotions function, and to safeguard against all excesses and distractions. Spiritual nurturing means awakening to our spiritual nature, and experiencing our inner essence and sacred spirit.

> *Life's experiences emanate from the One cosmic soul, which is both hidden and evident. We are driven to connect the visible with the invisible.*

6. HUMAN BEINGS

Paradoxes & Contradictions

Many of our endeavours are contradictions and absurd. We love comfort and ease, yet we carry on with actions and expectations that often cause harm and pain. We desire calmness and peace, yet we love excitement and extremes. Some people denounce religions, whilst others take refuge in them. Every minute we are closer to death and yet we desire longevity!

Supreme consciousness is the source of all life and awareness from which streams of consciousness emerge. Once one gives up the false identification of conditioned and personal biography, then most of these contradictions and paradoxes disappear and the light of pure consciousness engulfs us.

The body and mind validate what is transient and changing, whilst Truth or Reality is the only constant—this is the root of all paradoxes.

SPECTRUM OF REALITY

Change & Constancy

A child needs a calm environment to grow up in. For spiritual evolvement and transcendence, we need to be ready for a quantum change in mind and heart. A healthy mind wants to understand and connect cause, effect and different experiences so as to make sense of what may appear as random, chaotic and illusory. The mind searches for order. The heart and soul are the domain of the infinite that has no plurality of order or disorder within it.

We are frequently challenged in unusual ways, which cannot be understood by the mind and intellect. The heart has its own reason that reason knows not. All changes and earthly challenges will appear insignificant when related to the soul's perfect constancy.

Humanity wants to understand and relate via memory and experience, and spirituality belongs to a zone that is not subject to any limitations.

6. HUMAN BEINGS

Duty & Responsibility

Our sense of duty, responsibility, generosity, honour, loyalty and other qualities distinguish us from our animal tendencies of the lower self and ego. Liberation and freedom refers to liberation from the animal self in us.

Self-obsession and selfishness are basic survival behaviours, which are the obstacles for spiritual evolvement. Through empathy and service to others we progress spiritually to the doorway of awakening to Reality. Helping others whilst grooming the mind with loving intentions will allow the light of the soul to emerge and guide toward liberation. A healthy body, clear mind and pure heart are our primal duties.

> *For a child the ego is the friend and companion. For a mature person it is often the enemy. Through restraining the ego by kindness and duty to others we may transcend the lower self to soul.*

SPECTRUM OF REALITY

Love & Hate

Life is balanced between attraction and repulsion. Whatever has been conducive to good experiences and contentment is desirable and loved, and whatever is considered undesirable is repulsive or hated. Our emotions swing between like and dislike and other dualities.

Love emanates from the original source of creation and life with its qualities of peace, stability, connectedness and continuation. We love these qualities and hate their dark sides, such as enmity, discord, lies, hypocrisy and injustice. Love is like the river that leads to the ocean of cosmic consciousness. Kindness, empathy and love expand our capacity to experience the power of the present moment that emanates from Oneness.

All existence is balanced between what is admired and loved and what is detested. These dualities have their root in the sacredness of Oneness and its power of love.

6. HUMAN BEINGS

Levels Of Dependency

Everything in the universe is interconnected in obvious and invisible ways. All creations are related and are interdependent. A baby depends on its mother for survival. The mother too depends on others for help and on the baby for emotional satisfaction. All humans are dependent on air, water, food and energy.

The universe emerged from pure singularity and is dependent upon that original cause. The intellect discerns dependencies at different intensities and durations. There is a deep yearning in us to be independent or self-reliant in a durable way. We quest for the knowledge of eternal presence and the power of the sacred author of the universe. That is present as a soul within us.

Human life is based upon interdependence and yet we yearn to experience the soul's connectedness with the One beyond dependence.

Certainty & Higher Consciousness

The idea of security relates to dependence and independence. Human life is subject to agitation, change, doubts and frustrations. We hope to attain certainty and stability. Constancy, security and knowledge are the soul's qualities. Conditioned human consciousness is always insecure except for short durations that reflect the state of the soul.

Survival requires some stability and balance in the dynamic world of interactions and evolvement. What we can predict or control is a minor factor in existence. What is unknown follows its natural patterns and directions. Certainty is based on experiencing connected events. At higher levels of consciousness, we are close to the zone of soul's security beyond all doubts.

With full consciousness all is clear, while the normal human state is in flux and uncertainty—the nature of conditioned consciousness.

6. HUMAN BEINGS

Born Amongst Others

Humans evolve and develop in a social environment. Photons become particles and souls give rise to individuals with limited consciousness concerned with body and mind's survival. A personality, special identity or ego emerges when noticed and accepted by others.

Parents, nature and nurture play a big role in connectedness between head and heart, and the outer world.

With the development of senses, intellect and memory, we see differences and similarities between people. In our present world, the educated and upwardly mobile are at home among several cultures. This gives them a wider and richer share in life that can lead to higher consciousness and awakening to Reality.

Dualities emerged from oneness and human consciousness emerged from supreme consciousness.

Others' Faults

The mind naturally seeks out the exception—spotting change or the unusual and identifying faults or mistakes. We see what is unacceptable and is out of place. Survival and the norm dominate.

To recognize a fault in others means that we have that tendency within us. Impatience with others echoes impatience with ones own self. Whatever you witness outside of you, its intrinsic pattern resides within you. The lower self is driven to survive and maintain the illusion of independence; the more you attack it the more it will defend its illusory presence. You will forget the pain of a burnt finger but an attack upon your ego is long remembered and resented.

Defending the self implies looking for faults outside the self. No teacher, master or prophet was free of people blaming them and even accusing them of insanity! You will always find faults according to your judgement!

> *Teachers of wisdom and spiritual paths are often blamed by 'self-concerned' people for causing disturbance to the established order.*

6. HUMAN BEINGS

Stability & Prosperity

For survival we need an appropriate environment to interact with it. For growth and evolvement we need a balance between our physical, mental and spiritual states. The healthy home provides a certain measure of predictability, peace, nourishment, empathy and love.

For society to function well it is essential to have justice, peace, compatibility, cooperation and a will to prosper and evolve to better quality of life. Outer opportunities are necessary conditions for drives and ambitions, which ultimately may lead towards realising higher potentials. Therein lays the ultimate prosperity: experience of the cosmic treasure, the soul within the heart.

> *Outer reliability and security is a necessary background to the discovery of the innermost light of the soul—perfect and secure.*

Loyalty, Honesty & Reliability

For people to function and interact well with others, qualities of reliability, honesty, loyalty and other human virtues are necessary. The path of respect, justice, harmony, creativity and imagination leads towards higher consciousness.

The animal self in us presents challenges and difficulties which can be dealt with through upbringing, education and training. Grooming the self is to make it subservient to accountability, reason and intellect. The spiritual seeker will discover that body and mind are in an optimum state when constant reference is made to the heart and soul. Our life emanates from the soul, which is in unison with God and bears divine qualities and desirable attributes.

Honesty, loyalty, truthfulness or other admired qualities are human traits reflecting our soul's Reality.

6. HUMAN BEINGS

Creativity & Arts

We constantly aspire for higher levels of knowledge, consciousness and life experiences. The mind is the connector between energies and matter. We enjoy imagination, creativity and other activities that broaden and widen the scope of our consciousness.

Our mind deals with survival and the physical issues, and connects the physical world with that of meaning and the subtle realms. We are uplifted by listening to music that takes us into the higher and subtler zones of our creative potential. We find it tiresome to be caught in routine survival concerns. The physical world relates to cause, effect and plurality, whereas creativity and insights are closer to the light of unity and timelessness. Artistic activities enable one to drift beyond the normal mental limitations.

The sensory leads towards mental concepts, imagination and creativity—close to higher consciousness.

Fairness & Sympathy

The soul radiates life's forces and governs body and mind. Wisdom is fairness. A good judge must be fair. A reliable friend is fair. To understand your enemy you need to be fair otherwise you increase in confusion and discord.

Empathy is an expression and acknowledgment of connectedness. The self sees itself in the other's self. Physically mirror neurons are the basis of empathy and resonance with another being.

Sympathy is to reflect mentally pleasant emotions and feelings in occasions of distress and difficulties. It is an emotional act and can be potent with sincerity. The soul is the origin of such emotions.

> *Our universal origin of the soul is expressed in the human behaviour of friendship, empathy and generosity. Self-soul are inseparable during life.*

6. HUMAN BEINGS

Free Will & Determinism

Desire for freedom is a natural and forceful human drive of the self towards the soul. There are several levels and types of freedom. We desire to be free from physical pain or personal animosity and to be free to express thought and to exercise free will and choice. This is done in the hope of experiencing goodness, ease and contentment—happiness.

Existence follows countless patterns and laws. Outcomes are only predictable if we know all these variables. Every entity or system is also disintegrating and returning to the universal pool of energy. Personal destiny is experienced according to one's physical or mental connections in the pool of events. Our limited free will brings some partial liberation when we experience higher consciousness and the delights of the soul.

> *Desire for freedom can lead to contentment if we transcend the limitations of normal consciousness. Personal experience is dependent upon a viewpoint and the extent of consciousness.*

SPECTRUM OF REALITY

Pain, Pleasure & Lasting Joy

Why do we suffer? What is the cause of fear, insecurity, sadness or grief? How do we live in contentment? These are a few frequently asked questions. The mind connects the celestial soul to the terrestrial realm of the world of dualities. These realities exist and are experienced, but how real are they? Where are they when one is asleep? What happens to them after death?

We are conceived, born, grow up, become sensory-centred and identify our beingness with biography—all in the zone of pleasure and pain. Spiritual intelligence may take us beyond pleasure and pain to higher consciousness that is soul consciousness and natural joy.

> *Pleasure, pain, good and bad, and other features of pluralities are all earthly preludes to the realization of the soul and its joyful nature.*

6. HUMAN BEINGS

Denials, Deception, Concealment & Lies

Happiness and joy can be experienced when misery and depression are absent. Rejection defines what is unacceptable. Deception is a tool to escape opposition or difficulty in achieving an aim. Concealment and lies are also cover-ups to avoid censure or failures. All actions based on ego will carry some of these tricks and deviations.

We identify with biography and mind, desiring power and wealth and disliking weakness and poverty. Thus, we tend to deny and conceal what is considered unpopular and present an attractive face. The cosmetic industry represents the global art of concealment. The self itself is a fraudster. The sacred soul radiates its state through the heart as grace and self assumes the colours of these lights.

> *Our natural tendency is to be wholesome and real, as the soul is, beyond the undesirable states of deceptions and lies.*

Weeping & Laughing

Tears are the outpourings of emotions. They are usually an expression of grief and sorrow, but sometimes accompany laughter. Weeping can also be a result of anger, despair, pain or other emotions. Tears express emotional relief and release of toxins. They seem to be triggered from a zone which is between head and heart, and as such could be understood to increase the connection between mind and heart.

Weeping as a relief from past constrictions or sufferings is due to the joy of relief from self-delusions. Tears of sadness and grief may differ in their chemical composition from the tears of relief and joy—one is the expression of darkness and the other is light.

Weeping from sadness or joy are expressions of emotional relief and releases inner tensions and toxins.

6. HUMAN BEINGS

Sobriety & Intoxication

The mind connects matter and energy. The electromagnetic signals within the brain provide a means to an end. It is where the celestial and terrestrial unite.

A fuzzy, tired or intoxicated mind can cause confusion and harm. A calm, clear and healthy mind can better understand situations and function efficiently.

A sober mind is essential for human stability and is easier to transcend than a confused mind. Alcohol, drugs and psychoactive substances are risky substitutes for transcending the mind to the state of the soul. Intoxicants are like illicit entry to the joyful house of our soul.

To respond rationally to the world we need a clear and sober mind. For spiritual progress we need a pure heart and a taste of the soul's blissfulness.

Deception & Lies

Human cultures, religions and civilizations evolved because of the need to bring about harmony, justice and stability in human life. We are driven towards what is reliable and true so we detest lies and deceptions.

Part of anger against other people's lies and deception is against one's own self-delusions, false expectations and mistakes. It is challenging enough to deal with the ever-changing dualities and uncertainties in our day-to-day living, so to add it to it the human mischief of lies and deception is a natural cause for disappointment and anger. This is where we need to admit error and seek the light of the soul.

The force of repulsion produces anger and the force of attraction produces acceptance and contentment. Anger against injustice and human deception is an initial step towards witnessing truth in all events.

6. HUMAN BEINGS

Sadness & Gladness

Goodness and gladness accompany a relaxed state of mind. Our soul is the source of gladness and joy. The ego self, being the earthly shadow of it, is limited in consciousness and connectedness and is often in fear, concerns and insecurity. This is the cause of sadness and depression.

The path towards joy is to be aware of the causes of misery, to reduce desires and attachments and to constantly purify the heart and be at one with one's own soul. The development of this state of wholesomeness is the purpose of religions and spiritual practices. Sadness belongs to the ego self and gladness to soul.

> *We are attracted to people who are cheerful and avoid those who are miserable and sad. Our soul's nature is cheerful and light.*

Empathy & Envy

The feeling of loneliness relates to the self and ego. The soul is ever content and tranquil in its own perfect state. Empathy is a feeling that draws us close to others due to physical and emotional connections. Envy is a feeling that emanates from the ego as it competes with another's ego. It often produces sorrow or discord.

Empathy connects our mind with other humans, relate to innate forces of love and oneness. It expands our horizons and our universality, our mirror neurons resonate with 'others' and produce empathy. When energised by spiritual love, it leads to higher consciousness and lights.

The lower self is dark and tiresome, the higher self or soul is the source of light and delight. Souls unify and minds differ.

6. HUMAN BEINGS

Shyness, Guilt & Shame

Shyness is due to self-soul relationships. The light of soul brings shame and shyness upon the ego's conduct. Lack of full awareness at the time of an action is the cause of reassessment of past conduct.

The child's self-awareness develops due to reflections and corrections from others. The mature reflective being is between self-awareness and soul realisation. Remorse and self-correction are preludes to soul-reference. Our journey is toward experiencing the constancy of the soul's light: the one sacred Reality that gives rise to human reality. In that illumined presence, guilt and lower self shadows vanish.

> *Reflection upon emotional states emanate from the soul, which illumines the journey towards its own perfection.*

Generosity & Kindness

Personal identity, mind, and life's experiences establish and define humanity. This is possible due to our soul's divinity, which radiate higher qualities and virtues. Our soul connects the cosmic soul with earthly states.

Kindness and generosity are different strands of connectedness. These forces resonate at a subtler emotional level and connect the transmitter with the receiver. All our intentions, actions, hopes and expectations emanate from the source of Life within us— the soul via mind and intelligence. Human generosity is the outer overflow of the soul's quality of total generosity and unconditional perfect love.

> *Love of life, power, knowledge, ability and happiness are all attributes of the soul, and are transmitted to our body and mind, affecting our conduct.*

6. HUMAN BEINGS

Mine Or Not Mine?

We all claim some ownership or control over someone or something. This is a faint echo of the source that governs and contains all, on which everything else is dependent, in the world of dualities.

Territorial claim is a forceful feature in the behaviour of many animals. The force at the centre of a territorial claim is like the force of gravity—it draws to itself. Claiming control or ownership is an expression of connectedness and unity in a direct and personal way.

The self plays the role of control and ownership until it realises that, in truth, it is the soul that owns and controls on behalf of the One.

Needs, Thoughts & Actions

Most intentions and actions expect an outcome. There is a hierarchy of 'hoped' for or expected results. Basic safety, security, material and mental stability are at the foundation. Then comes desires for growth and development in the physical, material, emotional and spiritual spheres.

Outcome relates to time and place and is framed by its historical position. Every desirable outcome draws its energy from the source of life—ever-still and in complete peace.

The ultimate outcome is what is utterly perfect and is our essence, origin and source. The less are our needs, concerns and distractions, the more we experience calmness, clarity of mind and purity at heart. This increases the efficiency of actions and success in fulfilling needs.

> *On a cultural or spiritual journey, destination is connected with every step–the journey itself becomes the purpose.*

6. HUMAN BEINGS

To Find & Lose

We are relentlessly on the quest to discover whatever gives pleasure and satisfaction. We are always on the lookout for the philosopher's stone. We hope to awaken to constant joy. We seek what is unusual, new and exciting.

We detest losing anything that we considered ours. Some of us become collectors and spend much effort to secure and insure what has been acquired. Generally we are affected more by losing something than by finding or winning something. It is painful to lose what is loved. Yet most of us have not discovered the inner source of love—the soul within the heart.

> *Our human side finds and loses but higher consciousness has no experience of loss. For the soul loss does not arise. We quest for the state of constant perfection.*

Curse & Blessing Of Ego

Conventional esoteric wisdom advises control of the animal self and being critical of the ego. Numerous spiritual beings have labelled the ego as the main barrier to the light of the soul. It is more helpful to consider the ego as the lens that shows the colour of the pure light of the spirit. The qualities that we quest for are only discerned through mind and ego, like the rainbow colours emanating from the soul.

If you divide human life into three periods, the first third is for the ego-personality to develop, nourished by nature and nurture; the second period is learning from the pitfalls of the self, its assertions and delusions. With mistakes and suffering the mature person begins to experience wisdom and insights. The third part of the journey is to realise and live by the soul – a light that is the source of life and resides in the heart. Looking back, the ego seems a prelude to this welcome awakened state.

> *The ego serves its purpose by providing a cover for the sacred soul until one is ready for its light and presence.*

7. People

SPECTRUM OF PEOPLE

- ✠ Otherness And Oneness
- ✠ Earthly Stewardship
- ✠ Relationships
- ✠ Connection Samples
- ✠ Friendship, Companionship & Partnership
- ✠ Parenting
- ✠ Clans & Tribes
- ✠ Marriage, Intimacy & Sex
- ✠ Children's Spontaneity
- ✠ Social Groups & Communes
- ✠ Enmity & Friendship
- ✠ Dynamics Of Sharing
- ✠ Exclusivity & Inclusivity
- ✠ Making An Impact Upon The World
- ✠ Justice & Equality
- ✠ Respect Of Others
- ✠ Superiority
- ✠ Desire To Control & Dominate
- ✠ Status Due To Possessions

SPECTRUM OF REALITY

- ✠ Fame & Fortune
- ✠ Education & Upbringing
- ✠ Cosmetic Masks
- ✠ Am I Welcome?
- ✠ Part Time Life
- ✠ Playing God
- ✠ Sleepwalkers

Introduction

Since the beginning of the universe, matter and energy have increased in diverse qualities and quantities. Human life is balanced between qualities of humanity and threads of illumined divinity. By observing otherness and differences, and with insight and reflection, we may know and experience the essence of sameness and Oneness. Deep within ourselves, the souls carry a memory of singularity and the inception of creation.

The tendency to believe that more is better, together with our love for boundlessness, is an indication that Reality is beyond boundaries, and our journey on earth is leading us towards what is infinite and eternal. We compete and cooperate with other people, sometimes acting tough, strong-willed, and other times kind, gentle and flexible – all within specific limits, but aiming for increase. It is whilst being with other people that we discriminate between desirable and undesirable attributes.

Life's experiences have two aspects one is limited personal, bracketed between birth and death and the other reveals the truth of life itself, everlasting and cosmic. If one's earthly life does not lead to the cosmic reality permeating through soul consciousness, then our journey has been in darkness and accompanied by sorrow and grief.

The enlightened being lives on earth as it is part of the hereafter and thus is constantly revitalized by that magnificent realization. Every awareness of consciousness emerges from full consciousness which is boundless and eternal. The quality of life for any group of people is dependent upon the extent of reference to Reality and higher consciousness, reference, that is, beyond personal short term interests and survival needs. People are as good and wholesome as the extent of their higher consciousness and God's ever presence.

7. PEOPLE

Otherness And Oneness

The universe emerged from oneness and no one is excluded. Everything in it represents or experiences an aspect of Oneness. That knowledge explains the grief of the mental illusion of separation and 'otherness'.

All dualities, pluralities and opposites have meeting points in unity. Movement originates from stillness. Energy is the reality of matter and all possible times are eternally present Now. Natural laws of biology and other sciences are like veils over unity. In truth, timeless unity is what holds existence and its framework of space and time together. Otherness and multiplicity are rooted in Oneness and unity. In essence all people are the same. All souls have emerged from the same origin.

In essence, all 'other' human beings are the same as you— they desire ease, contentment and trust in perfect grace.

Earthly Stewardship

Some humans desire to rule, to be obeyed and followed. Some even imagine themselves to be God's chosen agents. Adam and his offspring are sometimes depicted as God's stewards on earth. The earth is a rare planet where life and consciousness appear in numerous diverse forms, expressing their presence in amazing ways.

Human consciousness grows and evolves from the sensory towards the higher spiritual realms, which encompasses other entities and existences. In this way, we carry the same root as others and thus have a duty towards all. The potential of enlightenment brings about inner freedom and outer responsibility—such a being will resonate with The Cosmic Author—The One.

Human consciousness dictates awareness, reflectiveness and reference to eternal consciousness and that is the foundation of stewardship.

7. PEOPLE

Relationships

Enemies neither relate, nor communicate. Friends connect, share and communicate at several levels. Lovers connect and resonate often beyond words and sounds. Hearts connect invisibly and then may express it. As for those in the ocean of Oneness, there is only rejoicing. They are at One. That is not an issue of relationship!

From earliest awareness, human life is an exercise to connect and unite, or to reject and avoid any connection. Our outer relationships involve the physical and the mental. In reality, the Source is the energy field emitted from the soul to bring into harmony all aspects of the self, mind and heart.

When the self is in unison with the soul, all relationships fit in with ease and efficiency.

SPECTRUM OF REALITY

Connection Samples

The universe is interconnected through countless forces, which we categorise as physical, chemical, biological, electromagnetic, gravitational etc.

Consider a mother's intuition and her ability to connect with the state of her baby. She also connects with it at physical and emotional levels.

The electromagnetic field emanating from the human heart is the source of electron movement within neurons.

Post-modern man also connects at multiple levels in the hope for a better life. The internet, telecommunications and other high tech connections are key aspects in our modern lives. A few decades ago, it was mainly through transport and letters. We strive towards instant connectedness—constantly.

The universe is interconnected and is rooted in its original singularity. Our bodies, minds and souls are connected and message each other.

7. PEOPLE

Friendship, Companionship & Partnership

Friends, family and society will influence us according to their ideas or values in what is considered to be real and what is false. A childhood friend might enhance the lower self; this may be enjoyable for a short while, but is a distraction for healthy evolvement.

A partner who enhances human or spiritual quality reflects the path of awakening and enlightenment. Early distractions and unhealthy habits can retard the natural growth in consciousness, mindfulness and free spiritedness.

Every person can be a mirror to the other. Your life's journey is through halls of mirrors. Hopefully you emerged wiser and less self concerned.

You will know a person better if you know his friends and associates. People reflect each other.

Parenting

Reproduction and parenting are expressions and manifestations of continuation. Parents pass on genetic patterns to their offspring as well as cultural and other unconscious influences. The outcome is a continuum of nurture and nature interacting. The body and mind are adaptable and are concerned with survival and ongoingness. The soul is the Reality that is perpetual.

Intelligent parenting implies training the child to have a healthy body, a well-developed mind and a natural disposition towards higher consciousness and the quest of the spirit within. Fortunate is the child equipped with outer and inner technology.

> *A natural parental hope and ambition is for their offspring to be better equipped for a happy life and contentment at heart.*

7. PEOPLE

Clans & Tribes

Human intelligence and consciousness emerged and evolved within families and groups. Consciousness expands and deepens when people bond together at different levels in relationships. With a reliable social foundation, you naturally explore other factors that bring about new discoveries and knowledge, thereby expanding consciousness.

Life began within a semi permeable cell which soon multiplied. The deep, creational memory of unity manifests as love and solidarity within a family, clan or a tribe. Hundreds of wars carried with them the idea of unity among people, which may include different races and ethnic groups.

Global professions and industry have reduced reliance upon family or clan. Yet there is always a natural drive towards our spiritual root and origin within the heart. That is the source of our love of family and tribe.

> *Physically we relate to our biological roots, spiritually to our original timeless Reality—ever-present at heart.*

Marriage, Intimacy & Sex

Marriage is an attempt by two beings to experience intimacy, love and connectedness, in body, mind and heart.

Over the centuries institutions and customs of marriage have changed in most cultures and religions. With the emancipation of women, their education and wider participation in social, economic and political life, the tradition of marriage has changed. It will change even further.

When sexual intimacy is founded upon unison in mind and heart, it will endure and lead to spiritual closeness. Sexual intimacy nowadays often serves as a release of frustration and satisfies animalistic conquest, often causing disappointment and confusion. The soul is sacred and so is the body by association. Legitimate intimacy can open the heart and lead to soul consciousness.

> *If sexuality is not due to physical and mental unison, then the harm it causes is greater than its short-term pleasure.*

7. PEOPLE

Children's Spontaneity

Children are often described as innocent, which is actually an undeveloped mind. Thus most actions are random, spontaneous and egotistical. Real spontaneity is what is emitted through the pure heart. The soul's light is ever-fresh and potent.

A child expects immediate fulfilment of any desire. With growth and grooming of emotional intelligence, patience for human limitations and understanding sets in. Yet we tend to emphasise the development of mind only. Childish spontaneity is then overridden by day-to-day needs of survival. For spiritual intelligence, early creativity may be helpful in later attempts to transcend the mind and senses. The seeds of spiritual awakening can be sown in childhood through creative wonderment, love and generosity.

> *The awakened person maintains youthful spontaneity and flexibility due to constant reference to the perfect soul within.*

Social Groups & Communes

Social life is necessary for human survival and for consciousness to expand. To be loved and accepted by others is important for growth and maturity. We like to connect with whomever we consider strong, intelligent, or attractive.

The self is driven to connect and continue until it is in unison with its soulmate at heart.

Family, clans, or communes are stages of belonging. Then comes the nation and humanity. We belong to numerous levels and zones of connectedness ending up where it all began – the sacred Oneness.

> *Attraction to the mother, parents and then other people leads to association with larger groups. The enlightened being is at one with the original light and source of all.*

7. PEOPLE

Enmity & Friendship

We prefer friendship to enmity. Attraction is preferred to repulsion. Gatheredness is preferred to dispersion. We are seekers of connection and continuity. When enmity transforms to tolerance, acceptance and friendship, we have moved from dispersion towards gatheredness and unity.

Friendship journeys towards unity and enmity toward its opposite, dispersion. Friendship implies connection and the promised continuity of goodness. There are two types of friendship and enmity. At the basic level, friendliness is a body and mind relationship, whereas at the spiritual level friendship is to do with unison at heart and spirit. Enmity is also at two levels: the zones of body and mind and when hearts are dark. The arc of ascent of consciousness is from dualities to oneness.

For the pure-hearted friendship prevails; for others it is according to the chemistry of body and mind.

Dynamics Of Sharing

Human life can be divided into three time periods, the first being from childhood to adolescence; from being very self-centred towards being more considerate towards others and increasing awareness of conduct. The second is where the lower self refers to the higher self for guidance. The third is awakening to the soul and overriding the animal tendencies within oneself. Sharing experiences with other more accomplished people in each period is helpful and wise.

Human beings appreciate generosity and sharing with others at the material and mental levels. Our soul or spirit takes from the One source and gives life to creation.

It is human nature to share and care for others during ease as well as difficulty. We emanate from and are sustained by One.

7. PEOPLE

Exclusivity & Inclusivity

The idea of God's chosen people is deep within collective consciousness. Everyone is special in one's own view. A child needs to feel special and favoured. Identity and self-concern brings about ability and will to function and excel in the world.

Individual identity enables the self to evolve and mature to the point where it may experience aspects of the soul's reality within the heart. Wisdom, justice and equality mean similarity of souls and spirits. That light is exclusive to every individual—and every human being lives by it. The advantage of feeling exclusive and special as a child will be a handicap with maturity. Truth reveals universal inclusivity – oneness that envelops the seen and unseen.

> *The paradox is that the human soul is both exclusive (you have it) and inclusive (everyone lives by it).*

Making An Impact Upon The World

A remarkable human drive is to excel and be outstanding and powerful, and thereby influence and change the world to one's own liking. People with a cause will most likely experience setbacks and difficulties. Often these are blamed on circumstances or the ill will of others. The self is ever self-justifying.

Spiritual guidance can turn the ambition of changing the outer world towards changing one's own inner state—from self to soul. This may lead to a better understanding of the world and its numerous layers of realities. Thus one can help others more effectively—due to purity at heart.

> *The natural desire to change the world is a reflection of the need of self to yield and be transformed to soul. This outcome is greater than changing the world.*

7. PEOPLE

Justice & Equality

People normally expect equity, fairness, respect and well-beingness. Justice is at the root of human creation in that all souls are the same in potential and are to be regarded equitably and with respect.

The root of human illusions, imbalances and injustice starts with the feelings of separation of the baby from its mother and the human desire for independence. In the womb there is total dependence. The wise rely on interdependence. The awakened being sees justice and grace in all situations both outwardly and inwardly. All has emanated from the most Just: the One.

> *It is natural to expect fairness, respect and equity; selves and egos differ but souls are the same.*

Respect Of Others

Who are others? No two are the same, not even identical twins. We all have different fingerprints, yet all of creation is inadvertently on a path towards its appropriate destiny where otherness has ended.

Apart from genetic differences and environmental constraints, we share sameness in the inner drives and values. You may be polite towards others, but you can only respect them if you regard them as the same as yourself in essence, not better or worse. Everyone is striving toward goodness in body, mind, and heart. We are all the same in our hope and expectations of a good destination. To love and prefer others over one's own self is a great practice to transcend the ego and resonate with the soul, and its sameness in others.

When you respect others as yourself, you are in close harmony to souls and their sameness.

7. PEOPLE

Superiority

We consider intelligence and mental agility as superior to dullness and ineptitude. The drive towards excellence, perfection and the hope of attaining some recognition by others arises out of the quest to seek greatness and status. That is our soul's state.

Whatever we seek is limited and not sustainable. Nothing ever remains superior or important for long.

We are subconsciously seeking what is constantly in a state of supreme perfection. This superior Reality has given rise to the human soul, which we seek. We are obsessed with our origin whose light is the source of personal life.

The desire to excel in the world and to experience acknowledgment is an echo of the greatness and superiority of the nature of our own soul.

Desire To Control & Dominate

The outer world will never satisfy the ego self. Its nature is a moving shadow nestled in the light of the soul. Once the soul is within space and time it will have a shadow. Like a fire, the more you feed it the more it wants—such is the ego.

The self can never be content with anything that is measurable. Its drive to control is relentless and can only end with its death, literally or metaphorically, which is the abandonment of self-interest and the pursuit of unison with its soul.

Much human suffering comes from the drive to acquire wealth, power or influence, or to control and dominate. Soul consciousness is free of all these desires - it is in utter perpetual perfection.

The soul is in charge and governs the human being and its shadow is the self which desires to dominate.

7. PEOPLE

Status Due To Possessions

The ego identifies with whatever gives it status, importance and attention. Your address, clothes and accessories reveal your aspirations or status. A watch discloses a profile of your socio-economic status in a flash, so does a car, a diamond bracelet or a string of pearls.

Personal identity is naturally connected with appearance and the value of what we carry on us. To discover the state and quality of a heart is a challenge. Ultimately those who know have transcended otherness to the realization of Oneness. All human souls carry the same sacred imprint and, as such, our origin and destination are the same — ever-present within the universe and beyond.

Most common folk look for the price of things but are ignorant about the treasure and joy within the heart.

Fame & Fortune

We seek knowledge, strength, ability and other qualities considered necessary for well-beingness and happiness. Fortune brings with it power and influence. Fame occurs when others acknowledge your skills, abilities, beauty, and other desirable attributes.

Spiritual intelligence reveals that all actions emanate from one source, and all power or wealth is a sample manifestation of that unique one Reality. The awakened being experiences perfection in the present moment and is beyond any desire or hankering for fame or fortune. Our magisterial origin is the source of our desire for fame and fortune.

> *Our soul or spirit carries all the qualities of the cosmic source of the universe, including fortune, wealth and boundless power.*

7. PEOPLE

Education & Upbringing

Responsible upbringing, education, and induction into cultural norms are intended to bring about a better life for everyone. Reference to the ultimate reality —and reference to a sacred light for higher guidance – was often an integral part of education.

Philosophers, prophets and leaders in education emphasised grooming the mind to expand the intellect, whilst maintaining purity at heart and high spiritedness. There is total connection between humanity and divinity, but there is a general progression from physical youth to reflective old age—from the gross to subtle and from animal self to the soul. Education is to bring out the ultimate potential.

> *Parental upbringing and tuition are necessary for physical and mental evolvement —necessary conditions for spiritual awakening to Oneness.*

Cosmetic Masks

Beauty is an outer manifestation of excellence, goodness and harmony. Striving towards beauty can be diverted when its main concern becomes outer appearance. This human deception prevails when the self or ego dominates and there is little awareness of the soul's presence, its lights and perfect beauty. The self always tries to hide its natural animal tendency and to appear with the soul's virtues. Cosmetic masks may help to bring out inner beauty or they may be futile cover up.

When higher consciousness reveals beauty as an intrinsic quality of the light of our soul, then less concern will be given to cosmetic covers. Inner beauty will shine through.

When outer beauty is not matched by inner beauty, cosmetic decoration is mockery and deception.

7. PEOPLE

Am I Welcome?

The human drive to connect and continue is most noticeable regarding social acceptability, popularity and inclusivity. The Big Bang of creation emanated from Oneness before any differentiation, dualities and otherness. Our lives are the echoes of this Reality.

The ego self will be at ease and in equilibrium when it is in unison with the soul. The self always seeks inclusiveness and connectedness with that which is desirable. And that is ultimately your own soul. The self yearns to be welcomed and the soul is the most perfect host. The real you—your soul is ever welcome and welcoming.

> *Your soul gives life and energy to yourself; and when you realise this Reality then your emotional intelligence will be set alight.*

Part Time Life

Our earthly life is a sample and prelude to the next domain of consciousness—the hereafter. In that zone, the limitations and dynamics of birth, death and other dualities do not exist and we experience life in perpetuity. The source of life emanates from Supreme Consciousness —Oneness.

Due to the human composition of body, mind and heart, our consciousness is constrained by physical realities. We need sleep to restore harmony for body and mind; we are energised by soul, the ever-living governing source. The hereafter leads to the reference to perfect and perpetual source of life.

> *We make allowance for our earthly limitations whilst evolving towards our origin— boundless life.*

7. PEOPLE

Playing God

The notion of the Big Bang emanating from singularity is a helpful and useful idea. The infant begins to develop an ego, with a childish mind it expects whatever it desires to be fulfilled instantly. The young child's mind develops to interface with material realities and the senses.

The mature person learns not to play God, yet strives for excellence and perfection. The awakened person has emerged from the cocoon of identity and separation and experiences illumined moments and the presence of Cosmic Reality—God. The enlightened being looks at creation through the lens of Oneness.

> *Each one of us contains aspects of animality, humanity and a spark of divinity. At best we may reflect an aspect of The Real.*

Sleepwalkers

The herd mentality, collective consciousness and love of tradition are common conditions of most people. Old cultures and ingrained bonds, including religion, language and life habits, are barriers to change. So are self-concern and the obsession with survival. This renders most people tunnel-visioned, acting as sleepwalkers. Minds are occupied, bodies act like robots and hearts are dark.

The people of Rome were surrounded by fire and most did not feel the urgency to evacuate. The unfortunate voyagers on the Titanic believed in the unsinkable ship and the orchestra continued playing. The love for continuity can override signals and signs of dangers. Sleepwalkers, like zombies, do not read signs or messages.

No human being is spared from nature's generosity and from the shocks in life to wake us up to a higher level of consciousness and soul awareness.

8. Today's World

SPECTRUM OF TODAY'S WORLD

- Spectrum Of Today's World
- Introduction
- Urban Life & Wilderness
- Modern Lifestyle
- Aspirational Lifestyle
- Gender Unity
- Drugs & Alcohol
- Nihilism & Hedonism
- Development & Progress
- Science, Technology & Spirituality
- Wealth & Power
- Politics & Economics
- Gigantism
- Techno-Usury
- Violence & Brutality
- Weddings & Hope For Unity
- Sexuality & Desirability
- Dating & Mating
- Euphoria & Depression

SPECTRUM OF REALITY

- ✠ Social Networks
- ✠ Analogue & Digital
- ✠ Changing Fashions & Designers
- ✠ Birthday Celebrations
- ✠ False & Real Commemorations
- ✠ Health, Sport & Wellness
- ✠ National Unity, Prestige & Pride
- ✠ Welfare, Health & Education
- ✠ Freedom Of Expression
- ✠ Leadership
- ✠ Governance
- ✠ Insurance
- ✠ Job Satisfaction
- ✠ The Cost Of Free Gifts
- ✠ Too Good To Be True

Introduction

The present moment is the outcome of centuries of influences and interactions. The pace of life was slow and natural selection played its key role in shaping us physically and mentally. A century ago, food production and village life was central to most people's life. More than half of the world's population is now living in urban settings with challenges and problems that never existed before. The standard of living and material needs are such that almost everyone is involved constantly to be in state of well-beingness, physically or mentally with no energy for head or heart.

Science, industry and technology has many advantages in making life somewhat easier and less traumatic. Equally, the speed of change over the past few decades has affected severely our bodies, mind and the environment. We now have to plan for leisure time and holidays as antidotes to the speed at which we are normally subjected to mental and physical stress. The world now is a far more ordered place, and laws and regulations govern almost all aspects of it—yet we cannot say that we are happier now than our ancestors were. In fact, the issue of happiness is very vague and resembles that of consciousness. How can you be happy without certainty of constancy? We have convinced ourselves that progress and development have given us greater control over our destiny and happiness. But am I happy at the point of death?

Many of our present day technologies are connecting the physical and the material world with that of subtle energies and transmissions. Within one century, we have moved from brutal force and heavy industries to fibre optics, lasers and many other subtle electromagnetic uptakes. From one point of view, technology may speed up personal experience of higher consciousness and transcendence of space and time. We are also dependent upon technology for the basic ease and comfort of our lives. We are living in a world where interdependence and connectedness are lateral and vertical across cultures and other boundaries. We may be at the tipping point of either being swamped by the animal self or by disciplines that help to silence the mind and experience the bliss of presence.

8. TODAY'S WORLD

Urban Life & Wilderness

Life has emerged from vast galactic outbursts and we carry some traces of the original wildness and explosiveness. Since the time of agricultural settlement, we have tried to combine comfort and ease with some exposure to wildness, or interaction with wilderness. Experiencing the wild is deeply engrained within us.

For centuries, there were cycles of urban dwellers being overwhelmed by wild nomads or hunter-gatherers, often in a pattern of three to five generations. With each cycle these raiders settled and after a few generations the modified cycle would repeat.

The experience of complete consciousness overrides the need to balance between urban life and wilderness. There is a drive for spiritual transcendence of normal consciousness.

> *Humans have emerged from wildness and are now in need of rising to a higher level of awareness that will neutralize sedentary life.*

Modern Lifestyle

Our highly regulated urban life is based upon competitive skills, professions, trade, business and industry, as well as sports and culture. Ancient values of hunting and gathering have morphed into shopping, clubbing and other social activities. Our lifestyle has evolved much faster than our biological and emotional growth: the emotions of a caveman hurtling in a spaceship.

We are connected globally through social media and other information networks as well as culture, commerce and education. Our aspirational lifestyle is balanced on the triad of consciousness, connectedness and continuation. When outer experiences lead to inner constancy and presence, we have moved towards completing the experience of total consciousness.

> *Lifestyle is durable if it enhances the permanent. Much of our modern way of life is a distraction and part of the feel-good attempts.*

8. TODAY'S WORLD

Aspirational Lifestyle

We all aspire towards a better life. We desire good health, wealth, good relationships, and presence of mind and heart. We love beauty, harmony and lightness in spirit.

We often imitate the lifestyle of whomever we admire. Popular leaders can inspire people with good conduct, such as patience, generosity, magnanimity and kindness. You can acquire some of those qualities even if you simply imitate your hero; through practice you may subconsciously achieve some of them. We influence each other on many levels and to different degrees. We are always aspiring to a state that is constant in its goodness and delights. We strive to live as a soul without the shadows and confusion of dualities.

The wise aspire to connectedness with a state that is constant, beautiful and perfect—the soul.

Gender Unity

Human experiences are within pluralities. There is no day without night, no pleasure without pain, no male without female. Man and woman complement each other and their marriage symbolises complementarity and union. We seek Oneness in all of our endeavours.

Outer differences are inseparable from inner sameness. Man and woman are similar in their innate desire for an awakened and illumined heart—peace, tranquillity, joy and happiness. The essence from which every being had emerged is the same and therefore ultimate destiny is the same. As such, we can only celebrate gender unity which is attractively wrapped up in contrasting duality.

> *Your mind tells you that you are different, so does your body, but your heart sings the song of Oneness. Outer differences veil sameness.*

8. TODAY'S WORLD

Drugs & Alcohol

A few centuries ago as part of our diet we ingested many herbs, fruits and roots which no longer remain easily available in many parts of the world. Psychoactive substances have been routinely used by human beings and for their domestic animals. Diet and nutrients often included berries, grass and flowers, some of which are now considered poisonous and banned.

At the end of the harvest of fruits, much of it fermented naturally and was used in villagers' celebrations. A millennium or so ago, the art of distillation of alcohol became familiar. Apart from its specific judicious use in medicine, alcohol's side effects are far more detrimental than its benefits. The same applies to psychoactive substances. The human desire for oblivion or transcendence is evidenced by the popular consumption of intoxicants. The natural drive is to go beyond the mind: not by numbing it but by transcending it to Soul.

The desire for alcohol and psychoactive substances is a manifestation of our innate drive to go beyond all limitations to boundless joy.

Nihilism & Hedonism

Real success is awakening to optimum consciousness and presence of heart. Nihilism ignores the idea of a higher purpose or direction that may bring about relief and new states to mind and heart. Cynicism and scepticism are part of that grim family.

Hedonism is a temporary escape from accepting boundaries, responsibilities and the limitations of body and mind. It is where adults pretend to be children, assume outer freedom and revel in the illusion of following what the senses, body and mind desire. The antidote to these situations is the taste and experience of spiritual awakening and joy. Following mental fantasies will lead to dead ends, but following the heart and soul leads to realising perpetual life and consciousness.

> *The awakened being is obsessed with being alive by the light of the soul, whilst acknowledging the boundaries of body and mind.*

8. TODAY'S WORLD

Development & Progress

It is human to hope for a better life and pursue ideas and plans to the end. But what is the end? The ideas of development and progress have taken on a life of their own. Most of our projects are based on outer concern for material progress and improvement in our physical and mental circumstances. There is little concern for our own spiritual well-beingness and liberation, as these are not quantifiable or tangible.

Developing our living environment can be at the cost of our spiritual well-beingness. So too the earthly delicate eco-systems are as much disturbed as our personal states. We normally consider growth, development and increase in wealth and prosperity as desirable. We also regard shrinkage or reduction in the material senses as undesirable. These sentiments ignore our spiritual reality.

Our interest to develop and progress in tangible ways, are preludes to the hope of contentment and unison with soul – the ultimate progress.

Science, Technology & Spirituality

From the beginning of creation, complexity was always on the increase. The rise of consciousness and life on earth flows towards higher knowledge, awareness, and the experience of pure consciousness or spiritual awakening.

With the industrial revolution and the vast technological openings in the understanding of minute existences and immense galactic events, we are closer to quantum realities and total consciousness.

Our relentless drive to get beyond the limitations of space and time has shrunk space and we are edging towards the experience of timelessness and perpetuity. Science and technology began with mainstream physical, chemical and biological fields and now tolerate the spiritual and metaphysical fields.

Science and technology are natural drives towards discovery and knowledge. Ultimately we are seeking cosmic connectedness and Oneness—already given to us!

8. TODAY'S WORLD

Wealth & Power

The mind learns the value and importance of life, survival and growth. The mind relates to livelihood, security, comfort and ease. The self loves itself.

Wealth is a power that can reduce physical pain and misery. It gives pleasure due to the ability to acquire what is regarded as valuable. Money provides flexibility and ease as a medium of exchange but also brings with it egotistic tendencies, such as greed and the justification of aggression and harm.

Numerous industries are based upon fear of loss of health, comfort or wealth. Inflation is a natural outcome of the desire to pay less for goods and services. Outer wealth and inner wealth rarely meet in one person! Very few people are on the path of inner wealth—the Soul.

The self, which identifies with the body and mind, is always concerned with wealth, power and the continuity of habits.

Politics & Economics

Politics and economics are the two main engines that lead most nation states of our world today. The forces of material progress and the idea of self-determination and democracy drive political life. A few decades ago, religious forces played a key role in human life. This force is much weakened and is replaced by human rights, health, sports, travel, cultural and other issues.

Social sciences, numeracy and economics can be helpful tools to expand consciousness. Politics, leadership and good governance lead to destinies as befits their ideals. Ultimately, governance begins with self-governance and enlightenment about the real human composition and journey in life.

Good governance is inclusive, steers a course of moderation and self-reflectiveness, and responds to mistakes and criticism.

8. TODAY'S WORLD

Gigantism

Small may be beautiful but so is large. Our soul's consciousness is beyond limits. We are in awe of the vastness of heavens and the immensity of space.

Ambitions drive us to larger scale activities, greater power and impact in life. A successful business model may grow and reproduce itself globally in a quest for universality. The soul's nature is universal and cosmic and we try to replicate that state on earth through gigantism. Truth is bigger than any size and it is beyond the limitations of space and time—beyond measure.

The awakened being lives within sensible and wise limitations on earth whilst experiencing the limitless light of the Soul within.

Techno-Usury

Limited liability corporations, internationalism and regulating global trade are natural outcomes of the human quest for material progress via control and regulations. Big business gives the impression of immortality as it adopts and morphs into new ranges of products and services. Founders, directors and propagators of the activity retire and die whilst the corporation carries on.

Leaders create the future by changing the present, whereas managers maintain the present. Shareholders' interests can be short or long-term. A few well-established commercial, global entities, may embrace fashionable ideas, including environmental concerns. Economies of scale and specializations help in producing more affordable goods and services, but equally reduce opportunities for individual trading and entrepreneurship.

> *The desire for instant wealth and power is a powerful drive. The financial industry grows in complexity. Only few look for the treasure within one's heart.*

8. TODAY'S WORLD

Violence & Brutality

The love of power, wealth, status and influence are inherent in us. Our conditioned consciousness drives us towards acquiring these assets. As these ideas have no definable end, their quest will inevitably produce some discord, violence and brutality towards oneself and others. Conditioned consciousness and curbing the lower self or ego leads to potential resistance and even depression, unless it connects with the higher self and soul.

The self is ever agitated and discontented. Every one of us is a war machine at the level of our ego, and much of our intentions and actions are expressions of frustration and discontent. Unless we live as a joyful soul, brutality and abusiveness may prevail. Peace and joy belong to the soul.

The nature of the animal self and ego is to exercise power and dominance, which cause disharmony and violence—unless Soul guidance is followed.

Weddings & Hope For Unity

Our obsession with life, knowledge, power, ability, connectedness and other desirable attributes are discernible manifestations of our obsession with our divine origin. We have come from the One, are sustained by the same One, are governed by the One and will return to the One.

Marriage in today's culture is a product of urban life and carries much of that artificiality. It pretends to connect eternally, but that quality only belongs to your soul, and not to your body and mind. As such, it is a reasonable pretence, if it leads to the realizing the One in you. All humans have similar souls.

We need partners; as a child, it has much to do with the body and mind, but with awakening, it is to do with unison between head and heart or self and soul.

8. TODAY'S WORLD

Sexuality & Desirability

Any consciousness, connectedness and intimacy that is durable, is desirable. We long for perpetuity or eternity.

The earliest memory of connection is between baby and mother. Then there are connections made through senses and body, followed by empathy, sympathy and other emotions, which can bring about closeness and love. Sexuality is an expression of a drive to intimacy at a bodily level, mental and even spiritual levels. If sexuality remains physical, it is short lived. We are driven to experience oneness and resonance with close friends and partners. The ultimately desirable is the ONE. Your senses, emotions and even hormones lead to connectedness and union, outwardly and inwardly.

Physical attraction is common. Mental, emotional and intellectual connectedness is less common. Spiritual links are most durable and can enhance both the emotional and physical.

Dating & Mating

As social beings we are continuously exchanging ideas, feelings, and knowledge with others. We love to explore new cultures, religions and life's experiences. We constantly seek balance and contentment.

Dating is a focused attempt to connect, relate, befriend and resonate at body, mind and heart levels—we seek unity. Mating is successful if it leads toward emotional and spiritual unison, growth and the experience of the lights and delights of the soul within the heart.

Outer dating and mating are durable and successful when the partnership leads to the realisation of your own soulmate.

Humans are driven towards higher consciousness. Most of our actions aim to enhance the state of our feelings and love. We are driven to experience our Soulmate!

8. TODAY'S WORLD

Euphoria & Depression

The soul's nature is blissfulness. Joy and contentment are qualities of the soul. We are recipients of these desirable energy fields but are distracted by the duality of our human existence. As part of our spiritual drive, our artistic and creative tendencies propel us to experience inner delights. A dark shadow, however, often accompanies these desirable moods.

Human consciousness spans across a very wide range of energy bands. The soul transmits total consciousness, modified through mind and senses, to become personal awareness and identity. Depression and sadness belong to the ego identity. Mental therapies try to relieve depression due to fear of disconnectedness or discontinuity. When the lower self has been contained, and sublimated to soul, sadness becomes a distant memory and bliss a norm.

> *Pleasure is accompanied by pain until we perceive existence through the lens of the soul—a steady state of euphoria.*

Social Networks

The drive for personal development and growth has become a global phenomenon resulting in a major industry in counselling and coaching. We seek unison with like-minded people and try to resonate and compete with increased connectedness in what is considered valuable and desirable.

Within the confines of personal and collective consciousness, there is a considerable advantage in temporary bonding and resonance amongst people; unless the multitudes of social media lead to the higher self and unity in essence, they will end up in the dustbins of passing fashions and herd mentality. The question is not the speed and the ease of connectedness, but the end goal. Souls are ever connected and at One, while the selves and egos are ever divided.

> *Like any collective power, social media can lead to mass euphoria and hysteria, but it can potentially also bring the mind to focus on its soul.*

8. TODAY'S WORLD

Analogue & Digital

From birth the human mind is trained to accept or reject; yes or no, breathe in breathe out, wake or sleep, match or mismatch. Our world lives by transmission and reception. This is the world of physics, chemistry and matter and diverse fields of energies.

The human nursery has to do with particles, and the life force provides a quantum field and wave functions. This is the zone of analogues and digital connectedness. Growth in consciousness implies the fusing of the world of the animal self and its dualities with the unitive field of the soul. We start attracting, repulsing and being digital. With spiritual nurturing we realize that our experiences are a small reflection of the boundless energy fields which envelop the universe.

> *The development of personal ego and identity is a starting point in the human plant growing from dark roots, to the ultimate flowering of expression of beauty and majesty.*

Changing Fashions & Designers

Humans respect time and thus love what is ancient, classical or timeless. We also love what is fresh and new. The cosmic soul is ever constant, eternal and perfect. As humans, we need fresh air to survive and similarly quest for freshness in the creative and unique.

Designers lead in presenting the unusual with confidence. When a designer combines a new idea with a touch of flare and uniqueness, it pleases the self and enhances identity. The quicker fashion changes the rarer it appears. We are always seeking the unseen soul – ever fresh, ever ancient and ever here, most rare and ever present.

Your soul reflects the sacred presence, yet your earthly side experiences life through change. The real you is eternal but appears changing.

8. TODAY'S WORLD

Birthday Celebrations

There is both virtue and vice in collective celebration. The virtue has to do with gatheredness and unity even when the cause is superficial. Communal activities produce some bonding and a sense of Oneness and ongoingness.

A few of us reflect upon the meaning of a birthday. You are now closer to death, so what are you celebrating? How much closer are you to awakening and enlightenment? If you are evolving spiritually, then that celebration is continuous for spirit has no end, but if you are celebrating only numbers of years, then you are deceiving yourself and others with noise and confusion.

> *Celebrations are two-sided: one is frivolous as it looks at the outer event without meaning, the other is acknowledging a natural unfolding to truth—this life is a prelude to the hereafter.*

False & Real Commemorations

Human life is a rehearsal for the return to the original state, often depicted as paradise. Our pleasures and celebrations are short lived and thus incomplete. Celebrating a birthday is like that, especially if the person is at an advanced age without spiritual awakening. When our earthly expressions of joy echo our spiritual reality then they are wholesome.

In the case of an old person's birthday, there is perhaps more cause for sorrow than joy if the end is near and they have not awakened to the perpetual perfection of their innate soul. Therefore, it is a false celebration. A real celebration is that which brings joy and is caused by joy and remembrance of mercy and goodness; the miracle of life is such an occasion.

The road sign to a city is not the city. Remembrance is a sign. Experiencing the light within is to be celebrated.

8. TODAY'S WORLD

Health, Sport & Wellness

For thousands of years our daily activities addressed our physical, emotional and spiritual needs. We are now specialists and need to give special attention to different facets of life that seem to be separate from each other.

We need to be fit and well in body, mind and heart. We have medicalized our health, industrialised our leisure and commercialised our wellness. We have produced specializations in every aspect of life, which may have increased pleasure as well as pain. We may be more efficient and materially more productive, but we have increased divisions and separations in our life's activities. Yet we desire holistic life and to be integrated and present. Today's challenges are complex and demand much attention. The real answer lies in meditative practices.

We exercise and pay attention to health and wellbeing and to have a healthy mind, which can be silent and content.

SPECTRUM OF REALITY

National Unity, Prestige & Pride

For a few millennia, human beings have been populating the earth in varied ways and situations. With the increase in human population, along with urban life, we have grown from being scattered tribes to being nations who vie and compete with each other.

Nations and groups of connected people often celebrate their uniqueness or other distinguishing features and group identity. However we may well have over-populated the planet and upset most natural balances. In addition, the symbols and trappings of being separate and special cause more imbalances. At least half of the nearly two hundred nation states are unstable and suffer from lack of basic needs, yet there is pride and celebration on national holidays. Irrespective of its suffering, nations try to put on an acceptable face and uphold a respectable identity.

To be proud and belong to a strong nation echoes human pride in being a soul that deserves respect and honour.

8. TODAY'S WORLD

Welfare, Health & Education

Within a few moments of birth the baby begins to express its needs and desires. Welfare at the survival level leads to growth in mind, intellect and higher attributes. Health has numerous aspects and we aspire to keep them in equilibrium. Education is the greatest asset for individuals and nations, for it implies knowledge and skills in the broadest sense.

Material, emotional, political and other stages of welfare are natural progressions towards a balance in well-beingness and fulfilment. The ultimate education is the realization of the cosmic Oneness and the unity between matter and energy; our limited mental consciousness is merely a prelude to the realization of universal interconnectedness and sacred Oneness.

Ultimate wellbeing is to know that your spiritual inner being embodies divine qualities and is not confined to space or time.

Freedom Of Expression

Every molecule in the universe has a specific characteristic which is disclosed as a frequency, along with other qualities. A flower advertises its beauty, scent and colour, and human beings naturally desire to express and share their state. With little encouragement a total stranger will express part of their biographical script. Self-disclosure is natural.

We feel deprived if restricted from expressing ourselves freely; our fear of rejection or punishment inhibits self-expression. Mental and spiritual evolvement is helped by freedom of thought and expression. To express and reveal an idea or thought may take us along to higher states of consciousness and awareness. Consciousness expands when interconnectedness is experienced.

The self is constantly evolving and changing; every cell or movement expresses itself and helps us move to the light within, which is the source of all expression.

8. TODAY'S WORLD

Leadership

The present moment leads to the next, tracing the arrow of time. The mother leads the baby towards stimulation and growth. The teacher leads the student towards new knowledge, understanding, and a better life.

Leadership relates to knowledge, competence and willingness to connect and continue towards goals and destinies. For specific skills within the physical and mental zones of life teachers and leaders are usually available. Leaders who can lead to higher consciousness are rare. Unless one has awakened to the inner leading light of the soul, leadership to higher consciousness is doubtful. The real leader is he whose soul leads him.

To lead towards a balanced human destiny one needs to be a follower of the soul and its divine guidance at all times.

Governance

Truth and reality is self-governing and self-sustaining. With reflection and wisdom, we realise that we are subject to a countless number of interactive forces. We are constantly interacting with our environment and responding to its states and stimulations.

Capitalism addresses the physical and sensory states of man. Communism hopes to stabilize society through collective development. Both systems promise to lead to contentment, happiness and higher human development. Communism was described as a natural outcome of the inequalities of capitalism. From nation states emerged welfare state and public capital leading towards more of a market and public driven economy with less government. Individual soul governance will being about a more just and durable collective governance.

> *The illusion of self-governance*
> *is the veil to soul-governance.*
> *Awakened beings bring about*
> *heavenly lights upon earth.*

8. TODAY'S WORLD

Insurance

The self seeks the constancy of the soul and looks everywhere in the world for it. We seek certainty in health, wealth, good relationships and enjoyable connections. We think, plan and act in the hope of experiencing contentment and happiness. Our highly commercialized world, which is concerned mostly with physical well-beingness, plays upon the usual fears of losing and failing and therefore we are presented with confusing choices from insurance schemes. We wish to live longer and have assured compensation for material losses.

Because we cannot forecast future contentment and happiness we are therefore mostly concerned with our physical, animal state. How can I tap into my heart's delights and joy?

It is the wise person who faces the questions: How can I be insured against misery and unhappiness? Where is my soul?

Job Satisfaction

Satisfaction and contentment in everyday life implies balance and harmony within oneself, as well as healthy relationships and connectedness to creations and the environment.

Whatever we undertake is an aspect of interaction. Repetitive jobs without knowing the final purpose are tedious. For a carpenter to fully enjoy his work he must know the wood he chooses, the different ways of joining and connecting, and then finishing, carving and polishing the final product. He then deals with customers who appreciate his skills and experience. A full cycle completed satisfactorily.

Job satisfaction implies placing one's job within its universal context. No matter what we do in life, if it moves towards the soul's cosmic origin and universality then satisfaction is more likely to be gained.

Fulfilment of purpose resonates with the already fulfilled soul.

8. TODAY'S WORLD

The Cost Of Free Gifts

Everything in existence is in balance. You exhale and inhale, you give and take, and these can be physical or intangible emotions.

Free gifts imply imbalance, which is not possible. So all gifts come with their hidden price tag but watch out for what is labelled as 'free' as it may be costly. Every cause will have an effect.

Helping someone out of your own volition does not imply the expectation of a tangible reward. Emotional intelligence drives us to be generous, kind and helpful. To serve or give, with no expectations has its own instantaneous reward.

The soul gives us life, which is the most precious gift, unconditionally. Kindness and empathy are steps to transcend the illusion of separation and enhance connectedness to original Oneness.

Many an enslavement has the appearance of goodness.

Too Good To Be True

Normal consciousness is a prelude to perpetual life and total consciousness. Exploring the amazing world of quantum mechanics, the common person may beg to return to the 'real world'. We consider the norm to be the challenge of dualities and hope for security and happiness. When you discover that the soul is perfection itself in perpetuity, you may think that it is too good to be true. The self tends to reject whatever is beyond its grasp and limitations. That is why belief, faith or trust is required to transcend the mind.

Truth is greater than any idea or imagination. When we are struck by an amazing event or insight that is beyond the norm, we may call it impossible or absurd. We are lulled by the ordinary and mundane!

> *What we consider true is a conditioned and limited aspect of truth itself. Truth is a quantum reality beyond mental grasp—it permeates all.*

9. Spirituality

SPECTRUM OF SPIRITUALITY

- ✠ Religion & Spirituality
- ✠ The God Question
- ✠ By God
- ✠ Everyone Believes
- ✠ Healthy Body, Mind & Pure Heart
- ✠ Cosmic Soul Within Earthly Body
- ✠ Most Rare, Most Valued
- ✠ Light Of Soul & Veils Of Self
- ✠ Soul Groups
- ✠ Types & Stages Of Nirvana
- ✠ Full Consciousness Permeates
- ✠ Quest For Mindlessness
- ✠ Sustainable Peace
- ✠ Earthly Transition & Transformation
- ✠ Prayer & Supplication
- ✠ Leisure & Meditation
- ✠ Activity & Aimlessness
- ✠ Reading The Moment
- ✠ Authority & Trust

SPECTRUM OF REALITY

- ✠ Liberation From Freedom?
- ✠ Baraka – Grace
- ✠ Generosity & Selflessness
- ✠ Lasting Liberation
- ✠ Reason To Live!
- ✠ The Four Journeys!
- ✠ Awakening
- ✠ Unified Dance & Dancer
- ✠ The Path, Discernable & Elusive
- ✠ Waking Up
- ✠ Teachers & Guides
- ✠ Religious Personae
- ✠ Spiritual Imposters
- ✠ Insane Or Genius
- ✠ Holy Madness

Introduction

The natural human drive to break boundaries and limitations is part of our innate quest for higher consciousness. The mind or self cannot be content except by the experience of the infinite and eternally perfect. When the physical and mental component of our existence is in equilibrium our quest for the subtler spiritual dimension becomes noticeable. The alternative is the futile obsession with material increase – in power, wealth and other illusions. The mind becomes more dominant while the heart remains dormant. Spiritual life is what is real and eternal. The young are preoccupied with the growth of body and mind and begin giving attention to the heart and its needs with maturity and wisdom.

Spirituality implies the essence and the origin of the universe, as well as our own roots and foundations. By nature we are spiritual, and cosmic consciousness covers a spectrum ranging from infinitude to that of conditioned personal life. The ocean and its droplets carry similar qualities.

As human animals, we experience limited consciousness and as souls, we are a microcosm reflecting the macrocosm. We carry within us the story of galactic events as well as the subatomic mysteries. Spiritual awakening will reveal boundless Reality. This state is the root of contentment and joy.

The quest for higher meaning, knowledge and spirituality is at the root of classical philosophies and religions. The path to that zone of beingness is based on realizing the illusion of selfhood and personal identity. We need the mind and senses for basic physical survival and earthly interactions. Yet, after this point, thoughts are a barrier to spiritual progress. Once you know you are not who you thought you were, you need to transcend the mind and biography to pure essence – out of the box of space and time. With this awakening your consciousness spans all earthly realities and the zone of boundlessness.

9. SPIRITUALITY

Religion & Spirituality

Earthly phenomena reflect heavenly realities. Religions try to describe and prescribe what may fulfil life's purpose and the balance between head and heart, and outer and inner states. Whenever a religion becomes established and traditionally embedded, it becomes part of a culture and way of life, and the spiritual dimension of a religion is weakened. Structured religion increases the power of a priestly class, who live off the common folk's ignorance, hopes and superstitions. Religious 'business' flourishes mostly due to fear and insecurity.

The dark side of religion can bring about extreme behaviour that may be in total contradiction with the original message and teaching. The essential original idea of most religions is to dispel ignorance and lead to a wholesome enlightened life.

Religion is a path that tries to explain human experiences and the ultimate purpose of life—awakening to truth.

The God Question

A few millennia ago the idea of a single God who governs all that exists gained acceptance in parts of west Asia. Debate and controversy continues ever since.

If God is boundless, sublime and timeless, then this concept cannot be understood by the mind, which only perceives definitions and differentiations.

Human beings aspire to acquire what was traditionally considered as divine qualities—power, wealth, and knowledge. The concept of God being greater than anything is a good start towards transcending the mental limitation of Godhood. A challenging revelation is that there is only God and all else are illusions of the mind and its limitations within space and time.

> *The big question is who and where is God? If the answer is that there is only God, then who are you? Even this question can only be posed by God's grace.*

9. SPIRITUALITY

By God

God, Atman, the Lord, Allah and other names represent the source of power, knowledge, ability, will and supreme consciousness.

To please someone is to bring ease and comfort to them. To please God is to know and live His will. To gain the colour of Reality is to enter into its sacred space. By God, anything is possible; by one's own knowledge and ability one is limited by perception and the basic forces on earth. God's knowledge is boundless but we function within limitations of time and place. God has no needs or desires and thus He is beyond pleasure or pain. People often use the phrase 'For God's sake', but it is not for His sake but rather, for the sake of one's own higher consciousness. We hope to awaken to divine Reality. Light upon light—The One Truth!

Reference to God consciousness opens up new horizons, invisible forces and power greater and subtler than discernible forces.

Everyone Believes

Our ideas about good and bad, and the past, present and future, are all based on belief. We do what we do because we believe that what we do will make us more content and stable.

With the advent of religions and the idea of a divine God, the Originator, 'progress' has produced a stream of religious paths. Hope, trust, and the desire to connect with infinitude, drive us all throughout our lives. We think and act due to expectations of some fulfilment—even subconscious by belief. The origin of belief is a light from the soul that activates the mind. An idea, a belief, trust and the experience of truth is the natural progression of belief and consciousness.

Without a measure of expectation or hope there will be little incentive to act. Most of us believe that tomorrow may be better than today.

9. SPIRITUALITY

Healthy Body, Mind & Pure Heart

When your heart is free from fears and concerns, the light of the soul shines through. A purified heart implies no hatred, animosity, anger or any other emotions that darken the light of the soul. Negligence of the heart's hygiene may cause darkness. There is nothing in the heart of the illumined being except the pure divine soul.

Our need for a healthy body and mind precedes the care and knowledge of the heart. Dealing with imbalances at the physical and mental level is easier to remedy than sickness of heart. Yet body and mind function only due to the generous soul—a sacred gift in the custody of ignorant humans.

We evolve from attention and concern for the body, senses and mental levels towards life's purpose—to experience the boundless life of the soul at heart.

SPECTRUM OF REALITY

Cosmic Soul Within Earthly Body

Your body is a temporary home for the divine spirit. Matter and energy have the same origin but appear separate and different. The soul's mysterious light appears in countless shades, colours and forms. The universe's diversity masquerades to entice us in discovering its original unity.

Separation and different identities act as temporary barriers that veil the light of the One. Body and mind veil your spiritual reality.

Beautiful objects simply announce their intrinsic reality—beauty. All appearances and objects announce their particular meaning and essence, an attribute of the original One. The same is true for your soul. What is needed is to hear its call and respond to it.

Your soul is sacred in origin yet it remains in its present, temporary residence in your heart. Be at its altar—worship and experience lights.

9. SPIRITUALITY

Most Rare, Most Valued

At first, what is important or desirable to us is mostly physical and material. Then come ideas and concepts such as love, freedom, equality, democracy, religion, etc. Then is the passion for the sacred and spiritual, which is most rare to experience – the mysterious soul.

It is natural that we are attracted to what is rare and unusual and to ignore what is familiar. In order to know the soul and its sacred precinct we need to leave behind everything else. The treasure of the soul is found when all else is lost. The soul is supreme. The One is true.

> *The greatest treasure is the human soul as it reflects divine attributes. It is most rare in the sensory world but shines in the unseen.*

Light Of Soul & Veils Of Self

To know your real self, stop the mind and listen to your heart—that is your soul, your real self.

The human soul with its desirable qualities energizes the physical body and mind. Your soul is your master and your destination; it spans all that is physical and metaphysical.

All sentient entities have a soul with a specific potential in consciousness. The soul of a mouse is more limited than that of a primate. The human soul resonates with other souls and is a like a holographic representation of the cosmic soul and is in total entanglement with it. Inseparable from its sacred origin, it emits the light of the One.

The nature of soul is primal light and its purpose is to illumine the physical and mental components of humans.

9. SPIRITUALITY

Soul Groups

There are physical, chemical and subtler similarities and complementarities in existence. Souls denote energy packages that give life to specific entities. The numerous species of ants have souls which can relate to other ants and thus can be considered as a group. So do many other sentient creatures. The souls of all human beings have the same potential as far as consciousness and higher reality is concerned. The selves, however, differ.

In creation, countless patterns and energies interact and connect. Most sentient and living entities are given life through their particular soul, which fits in within a wide range of spectrum or hierarchy. As such there would be numerous 'soul groups' according to species and types of creations.

Outwardly we are inclined towards similar people and connectedness with them. Souls are the same. They meet and resonate with similar souls.

Types & Stages Of Nirvana

People who are interested in spirituality are often curious about what is described as bliss, joy or nirvana. To begin with, the main concern of human beings is to reduce agitation, confusion and concerns of body and mind.

Least distraction of one's body and mental concerns implies being at the door of pleasure. Early humans spent much of their time idle and enjoying purposefulness. In our present complex world, we yearn to experience harmony and an easy flow of life. Some people can occasionally touch that zone, while others can plug into it firmly. Transcending identity and mind takes one to the gate of inner paradise.

> *Descriptions of happiness or joy can be misleading. Departure from conditioned consciousness towards ultimate consciousness is the path to sustainable joy.*

9. SPIRITUALITY

Full Consciousness Permeates

Our universe contains numerous fields of energies, some of which are branches and offshoots of others. All of these fields emanate from the original cosmic field of light and energy. Consciousness is one such major beam that connects with other fields. All life and awareness has emerged from one source which is the only perpetual reality. In our day-to-day life we strive towards that source, mostly subconsciously.

Full consciousness emerged with the start of the universe, perhaps one of the earliest fields of primal energy. Soon, both matter and energy began to fill space-time. Countless types and degrees of consciousness interact within the universe. As humans, we exercise a wide spectrum of consciousness that includes our physical, mental and spiritual aspects.

Consciousness of our humanity points towards higher spiritual consciousness within the spectrum of our sentiency.

Quest For Mindlessness

The mystery of life and consciousness remains the big question in our existence. Nowadays we visualize creation as having come from nothingness, the absolute singularity. Religious minded people often describe creation as the will of God and His generosity. Divine effulgence and grace permeates all known and unknown.

Mindfulness means clarity, focus and single pointedness. Mindlessness implies thoughtlessness and to be in oblivion. Both ideas relate to a state beyond the mind. The human composition of body, mind, heart and soul, point toward a process of moving consciousness from the terrestrial to the celestial, or from the ordinary to the extraordinary, from identity to Reality and from physics to metaphysics. This process is transcendence of mind and time.

> *We use many words to describe humanity, multiplicity, or duality, as earthly aspects of cosmic unity. To experience sacredness we need to transcend normal consciousness.*

9. SPIRITUALITY

Sustainable Peace

Peace is a divine attribute and is at the foundation of the human spirit. The slogan of "the war to end all wars" is a mockery of earthly reality and human nature. War is due to the animal self. Peace begins at heart and implies contentment due to experiencing of the eternal light, of soul. All human souls exude peace and love.

The original peace continues to live within our soul. That which was at the beginning, is still there and to it everything will return. In order to experience this primal peace, we need to get out of the shadows of the lower self. Darkness will vanish when identity and thought are transcended. All that remains is original, perfect, blissful peace.

Sustainable peace is the outcome if humans become closer to the peace of their own soul, and live in that state.

SPECTRUM OF REALITY

Earthly Transition & Transformation

Our journey is through separation, individuation, dualities and uncertainties along the path to the original unity. Our earthly consciousness yearns for its origin.

Wisdom is to seek Truth. Scepticism is to see the futility of everything. Illumination is to experience stillness and timelessness that underlies all change and transition.

We are challenged by the temporariness of our life and look for answers as to the real purpose of creation. The ultimate abode of contentment is when you experience life through your heart's light. Then, the transition on earth leads to transformation to the best destiny.

Our earthly experience is preparation for life after death as well as on earth—when we live as souls on a journey.

9. SPIRITUALITY

Prayer & Supplication

Why do we pray? To whom do we pray? Why are prayers so seldom answered? Yet we still pray and hope for a favourable outcome.

This deeply ingrained human need drives us towards higher consciousness and spiritual certainty. We are all dependent on the mysterious life forces to keep body, mind and heart alive and well — free from sickness, fear, anger and other emotional blockages.

Our natural disposition towards hope and a better future propels us to call upon the original cause of creation for guidance. Regular periods of seclusion and isolation may reduce our sensory dependence and enhance our transcendence in consciousness.

> *We are mostly material and sensory creatures that quest for subtle emotions, feelings and intuitions that transcend the physical.*

Leisure & Meditation

Life has emerged from self-sustaining consciousness. Forces that bring about wellness and balance propel the human journey. Once our basic needs for survival are fulfilled, we long for ease, comfort and leisure. We seek subtler experiences that transcend our senses and mind. Positive 'idleness', reflectiveness and meditation are what we enjoy and desire —spiritual holidays, leisure, a relaxed state of body, mind and heart.

Our life is limited due to conditioned consciousness and memory, yet we strive to prolong it, and to experience perpetual well-beingness and flow in time, without stress or fear. Meditation becomes transformative when attention and focus flows into boundless consciousness, without a goal or predetermined direction—conditioned consciousness yielding to its source and origin.

Our soul is eternal and what we aspire for at all times is to experience a state of blissful ease – a perpetual now.

9. SPIRITUALITY

Activity & Aimlessness

An impulse or will arises after stimulation. Intention, action and attention follow thereafter, aiming for an outcome. We love to leave a mark, an impression, or evidence somewhere, as an expression of having been here. The travelling monk leaves a flag on the mountain.

When outer activity is balanced with inner calmness and silence, then the outcome can be potent and effective. Humanity requires constant balance with spirituality. We are largely influenced by our earthly connectedness through our senses, memory and mind. With spiritual evolvement and the practice of inner silence and transcendence, we experience wholesomeness of Oneness—the real objective of life.

An active life requires health, ability and purposefulness, to be balanced by regular periods of stillness and contemplative idleness.

Reading The Moment

We respond to signals as we experience and grow in consciousness. The human microcosm is ever connected to the macrocosm in visible, invisible and entangled manners. Everyone lives a temporary identity, which evolves every moment.

Initially we read vague aspects of the moment. We respond to physical signs such as pain, pleasure, emotion, as well to subtler inexplicable signs. We grow from the physical, to the emotional and the spiritual. All of these states exist in the moment.

The full spectrum of consciousness in human beings connects physics with metaphysics. Tasting the infinite moment is the entry to the zone of complete consciousness.

The moment, the now, is ever perpetual and to read it is to open the book of cosmic truth.

9. SPIRITUALITY

Authority & Trust

There is an innate desire in us to trust. Most of us will have experienced mistrust and disappointment. How to trust? A few know to trust their heart. A few know not to trust the lower self, for it is most unreliable, deceptive and untrustworthy.

A child may put up with parental authority, but the adolescent often rejects and suspects outer authority. Rebelliousness accompanies the rise of intelligence. The wise adult may question the ego's false assertions and pretences. The enlightened one listens mostly to the soul's voice and authority.

The love of authority is the love of the soul. When one knows, loves, and follows one's soul, then one is truly trustworthy.

The author is One. Trust emanates from love and subservience to the One — ever-present but often veiled by the lower self.

Liberation From Freedom?

We relax when free from thoughts and need for action. We are driven to be free of pain, anger or injustice and other shortcomings. We quest well-beingness contentment, and ultimately the delight of presence. We are dependent on food, drink, air and other needs and yet we hope for liberation! What we really quest is ease at body, mind and heart. As long as we are alive, there is no total liberation or freedom. We desire to be as near as possible to neutrality, stability and balance.

It is only through reflective transcendence that we may experience another zone of liberation; this relates to oblivion and no-thingness. This is the higher zone of consciousness, which is our soul—ever free of needs and perpetually alive.

As humans, the quest for liberation is continuous, until the soul is experienced, before or after death!

9. SPIRITUALITY

Baraka – Grace

We always look for the extra—something more, a bonus, and a free gift. Outer needs may be satisfied, but not the inner. That is the domain of infinity.

Baraka is a perception and experience of the unexpected extra and unsolicited goodness that adds to contentment and gratitude. That experience has a special thrill in it. It comes with trust in the Perfection of the Real. You need to be ready to receive it. That requires trust, faith and purity at heart. The universe is suspended in Grace.

> *Baraka is the goodness that descends from the unseen to augment the seen. When you have done your best and trust in Grace, then Baraka is felt.*

Generosity & Selflessness

We enjoy ease and the smooth flow of life, welcoming generosity at all levels—material, mental and emotional. A generous act can be transactional or free of the expectation of any return. Even then, there is a subtle transaction—the giver also receives.

All our actions are interactive and the dynamics of energy fields and matter are ceaseless. A generous mind is limited and measured whereas a generous heart can be unconditional and simply flows. The ego self is the obstacle to such generosity and can darken the heart. Modesty reduces egoistic tendency and selfless acts touch hearts and souls. The human journey is from ego to soul.

The ultimate human purpose is to recognize the ego's limitations and transcend it through generous acts and unconditional love.

9. SPIRITUALITY

Lasting Liberation

The human desire for power and freedom is an attempt to improve on connection and continuity. The drive towards choice or freedom is a self-deception emanating from the animal self in order to prolong its illusory identity—a changing shadow assuming independence. The soul is free from the notion of limitation or liberation.

All notions of freedom are to do with the body and mind. The self desires freedom as an echo of the nature of the soul – ever-present, ever-perfect. When the nature of the soul is realized and experienced, then the desire or idea of freedom or choice disappears and what remains is blissful peace.

The quest for liberation may take us to soul consciousness, which is free from all human illusions and desires for liberation.

Reason To Live!

Our life today is purpose-driven because of the dominant material needs and goals we choose. Our society, in fact, undervalues those who live without obvious ambitions or outer aims to achieve.

If you are sane and not a hedonist and are courageous to question the reasons people present and give to justify their relentless ambitions, you may well be accused of being peculiar and eccentric. The teenager has numerous doubts and questions. Middle life crises often invoke the deep question of why one is in this world. The fortunate one will discover that life itself is the source of the entire universe and is worthy of unconditional love and connectedness. Life's reason is to transcend the temporary phase to the everlasting.

Our conditioned consciousness brings about changing reasons and quests in life. The light of supreme consciousness declares itself as the reason.

9. SPIRITUALITY

The Four Journeys!

There are numerous descriptions of the human journey on earth. The four journeys is one such description. The first journey is turning away from creation towards the Creator. The second journey is being at the Godhead with no thought, no mind and no identity. In this state, there is only oneness. The third journey is from that sanctum of absoluteness towards what emanates from it—pluralities and otherness: from God towards creation. The fourth journey is to be amongst creation but with the heart and soul completely at One with the Creator—witnessing multiplicities while experiencing unity.

All of us at one time to another experience an aspect of these journeys.

The first journey is common. The second is rare. The third is rarer. The fourth is least traversed. The journey towards ultimate union moves along steps and stages.

Awakening

Truth is ever there—permeating the universe. It is dimmed and masked by our mind and memory. This majestic Reality is the cause of all existences and consciousnesses. The light of truth was already there, before time or the emergence of creation.

As part of evolution conditioned consciousness had to be prepared and readied to experience its magnificence. The experience of isolation, separation, bewilderment and confusion will continue, until one leaves the desert of desperation. Then the mind may be still and the heart beams its light. The realisation that there is only Oneness and no otherness is awakening. Then personal will is experienced as a distant memory. Everything loses its significance. Only the light of presence is ever effulgent - Truth.

All life's experiences lead us away from shadows and illusions towards the cosmic light, towards awakening.

9. SPIRITUALITY

Unified Dance & Dancer

Connection, resonance and unity are essential drives in human life. Dancing is the response of body and mind to attractive rhythm and harmony. The dancer's desire is to transcend the mind, normal consciousness, identity and self-awareness.

The rhythm and its impact upon normal awareness take the dancer to a state of obliteration with the dance. A good dancer who practices and trains seriously will go past awareness to reach top performance. The great musician loses self-awareness to the music. The dancer unifies with the dance and both vanish into the mystery of the harmony of sound. When the self is diminished, the soul is evident. When identity is lost the beauty of Reality appears.

To find your real self —your soul— lose your identity and yield to the inner light of your soul.

The Path, Discernable & Elusive

The child's mind develops with imagination and actions. For the young everything may be possible. Experience, reason, logic and intellect will narrow possibilities and interests. Our drive for freedom enables us to choose, sometimes rightly, sometimes wrongly. With wisdom choices become only what produces goodness that lasts—a narrow path.

The awakened being disdains choice. Spiritual wisdom requires the optimum at all time — illumined presence. From a wide range of choices to no choice—flowing with light—presence in the perfect now. There is one perfect choice at any time—that is the path of perfect flow.

With awakening we follow the one and only optimum choice. The path of knowledge ends with the end of personal will or desire. The path was the excuse to leave illusions of dualities behind.

9. SPIRITUALITY

Waking Up

Truth is not subject to change. It is constant and covers all that exists in the universe. Realising this majestic Reality is like waking up from a dream. The dream, as well as the waking state, is the illusion of the mind. Reality is the only Real!

The light of lights was always there but we have to be prepared in order to experience its magnificent effulgence. Isolation, separation and bewilderment in the endless desert of the fantasy of otherness are often necessary preparations. When the mind is still and the heart is pure, the realisation of what had always been becomes obvious: Oneness and no otherness, One Cosmic light and countless shadows. Old experiences seem as distant dreams bearing little significance. Only the light of One is ever-present.

> *Everyone strives to discover Reality and be content. There are different levels of spiritual experiences all leading to inner stillness and pure witnessing.*

Teachers & Guides

We naturally desire to know, discover, understand, and become powerful and able. We strive for higher consciousness and greater perception.

We learn from the past and from those who are ahead and more skilled. In a way, everyone is a teacher and is also taught. The most important aspect of learning is that which improves a sustainable quality of life and provides the knowledge of the basic forces and maps of Reality. Teachers of skills and sciences are necessary but more important are spiritual guides and companions. These are rare in today's world and difficult to find out and to evaluate.

Guidance may come to you in multitudes of ways. In the past, teachers had clear roles. Now you can learn from an ant. Nevertheless you still need a being who reflects your ego-self. The self is a treacherous impostor.

Philosophers were once regarded as teachers of the meaning of life, then religious leaders were, and now there are no clearly defined guides as such.

9. SPIRITUALITY

Religious Personae

Human beings cannot live or flourish in isolation. During adulthood, some people benefit from periods of seclusion and isolation. What a difference between enjoying being alone and feeling lonely. Being alone is to exclude intrusions. Feeling lonely expresses the need for companionship.

Material and physical powers enhance the ego. Religious power is more dangerous: it can cause greater damage than the trader who lies or cheats in his worldly transactions.

A few suspect spiritual teachers may demonstrate their power with miracles and magic. The real master is he who helps you reach your own inner mastery, free of dependency on any outer state or knowledge.

Religious status can benefit or harm. A pious personality might be more veiled from Truth than a dejected villain.

Spiritual Imposters

The human drive towards wider horizons and greater knowledge is relentless. Traditionally religious or spiritual people were considered of higher moral quality, generosity and love. This assumption renders religious or spiritual imposters as a human disgrace. Often priestly competition, slanders and attacks are disguised by polite behaviour.

Even worse is when such imposters abuse their status, especially amongst novices. The damage can be more than physical or mental. It diminishes humanity and obliterates spirituality.

A human being can be abusive and egocentric at any time in their life. The body may heal quicker than the mind, and the mind may heal quicker than the heart. And the heart knows.

9. SPIRITUALITY

Insane Or Genius

Past memories, traditions and collective consciousness are the usual reference points of what we consider normal or not. Anything that is outstandingly different to what we are used to can be considered as inappropriate, wrong, stupid, or just plain insane.

Many prophets, great thinkers and geniuses have been considered mad, insane, strange or eccentric. Evolution and progress in life is slow and incremental and anything that is radically different is often disregarded or rejected as wrong, unacceptable, irrational or mad. Supreme consciousness is ever supreme.

> *There is a thin line between insanity and genius. Neither state follows the mental norms or conventional values and habits.*

Holy Madness

The definition of sanity is to understand the world and interact with it. The many dualities: energy and matter, seen and unseen, are in perpetual dynamic flux. This is considered normal and healthy—making sense!

It is natural for us to judge and evaluate within a norm. There are always people whose consciousness and behaviour doesn't quite fit. Some of these beings are within zones of consciousness not easily understood or defined. Some are near enlightenment and some are closer to states of mental fluidity.

Spiritual insanity is a state in which you do not experience perpetual boundlessness, which is the primal and original state from which the universe had emerged and is suspended in. The human soul carries that imprint.

> *Human sanity is to think and interact through reason and intellect. Spiritual insanity is to be confined to that restricted state only. The human spirit is eternally boundless.*

10. Guidance

SPECTRUM OF GUIDANCE

- Cosmic Will & Destiny
- Worldly & Spiritual Guidance
- Humanity & Universality
- Personal & Collective
- Persistent Quest
- Stages Of Migration
- Inner & Outer Change
- Resistance To Change
- Breaking Habits
- In Tune
- Heart To Heart
- Enter Through The Door
- Suffering & New Openings
- Guarding New Openings
- Divine Attributes
- Fear Of Provision Or Creation
- Sorrows, Fears & Expectations
- Who Is Your Teacher?
- Following Instructions

SPECTRUM OF REALITY

- ✠ Steps To Awakening
- ✠ Mindfulness & Mindlessness
- ✠ Judge, Repent & Witness
- ✠ Self-Punishment
- ✠ Serving Others As Yourself
- ✠ Appropriateness & Context
- ✠ Morality
- ✠ To Mimic & Admire
- ✠ Love As A Climbing Rope
- ✠ Present Presence
- ✠ Relief From Envy & Jealousy
- ✠ A Remedy Or Poison
- ✠ Ego As Foe & Old Friend
- ✠ Condemn The Action Not The Person
- ✠ Sublimate Major Problems
- ✠ Moderately Extreme
- ✠ Watch For Excess & Waste
- ✠ To Be At One Follow An Enlightened One
- ✠ Reliance On The One

Introduction

We need help, assistance and friendship to survive. Without help, empathy and love, human life will be barren, crude and brutal. Guidance is like a beam of light which, when followed, will help make the journey safe and pleasurable.

Knowledge and experience leads us to understand our human make-up and its evolvement. Relevant guidance will enable us to access the intellect and refer to the higher consciousness of the soul. Guidance comes with the hope that tomorrow one may be in greater ease, contentment and happiness.

We need health and harmony at the material, physical mental and emotional levels. With maturity, we need spiritual guidance to access our own soul and heart.

The need for inner and outer reference and guidance is constant throughout life. As all human experiences are part of the dynamics of duality, there is the need for connectedness to guidance, inspiration or reflection. An outer warning signal stimulates an inner receptor, and the outcome is a rapid move to avoid danger.

Good guidance is that which is appropriate at the time and place, leading to a more evolved state of greater knowledge and wisdom. Our journey in life is but a drive towards full consciousness so that we are cheerful and content at heart irrespective of outer circumstances.

SPECTRUM OF REALITY

The most valuable guidance is that which leads to discovering who one really is. How to avoid fears and anxieties? To regard death as a friend! To live fully in the present! To awaken to Everlasting Reality.

10. GUIDANCE

Cosmic Will & Destiny

We desire to express ourselves and pursue personal will. The wise one will try to fit his will within the cosmic will. How to understand God's will and be in harmony with it, is the big question.

To know God's ways or Cosmic Will, we need to transcend all thoughts and personal will. All forces and powers emanate from One and are filtered through different levels of consciousness. Personal will is a small part of destiny. We cannot control the outcome of events and their effect upon our contentment or happiness. God's will includes personal will and countless other wills and forces, seen and unseen. The intelligent being hopes to make personal will part of God's will. That is enlightenment in action. Human life illumined by God.

What will prevail is the combined outcome of countless forces and hopes. To be in the Now is to be least attached to transient states.

Worldly & Spiritual Guidance

There are two levels of guidance. One is to do with the world of dualities and physical and mental states. The other relates to heart and soul and awakening to higher consciousness and grace. Worldly guidance changes according to the circumstance and the need to bring equilibrium and harmony to body, mind and heart.

All worldly guidance and wisdom is a prelude for higher spiritual guidance and experience. Spiritual drive is the force behind existence and leads back to the Source. The most durable and sustainable guidance is that which elevates our consciousness towards its supreme light.

> *The natural outcome of knowledge and guidance is the experience of sacred presence and its perfection.*

10. GUIDANCE

Humanity & Universality

The quest for that which is higher, bigger and infinite is part of the natural drive towards higher consciousness. Expansion and diversity is the natural order of our life. Gene pools improve by cross cultural and racial marriages. Stagnation and preservations are not conducive to the flow towards boundlessness.

Individuals who have transcended their parochial, racial and cultural backgrounds will have advantages in the global culture of today. The cosmic reality of the human soul radiates forces of expansion at all levels of human existence especially concerning wealth, power and knowledge.

The universe is ever expanding and so is human consciousness, along the path of ascendance toward the natural destiny of boundlessness.

Personal & Collective

Conditioned consciousness and the metaphor of the fall of Adam, is balanced by the human quest of higher consciousness and boundless goodness. When the individual and the collective are in harmony, then humanity and divinity are closer in balance. Ultimately, what is good for individuals is good for the community.

One can neither deny individuality and the personal drive for durable fulfilment nor deny empathy, sympathy and the universality of the inner drive within each one of us. The microcosm is in balance with the macrocosm at all levels.

Evolvement implies being friendly and resonating with others. Your journey in life can be occasionally lovely and at worst times with others sharing and caring.

> *The individual soul brings life to the body and mind, but as all souls are similar, we are naturally driven towards others.*

10. GUIDANCE

Persistent Quest

Human life is filled with challenges, difficulties and uncertainties. We begin with simple childish issues and end up with the primal question of 'Who am I?' and 'What is the purpose of life?'.

There are of course several levels to our concerns. For a teenager the mind is still developing and interaction with the heart is fermenting. With old age, unless self-soul balance is established, depression, darkness and fear of death may dominate. The earlier in life one seriously considers the Big Questions, the more is the likelihood to reach the head/soul balance and experience higher consciousness and spiritual vistas.

The door to these answers is beyond ego identity and human concerns. It lies within the soul at heart.

> *Expect goodness in every situation in spite of your judgment or the outcome; you may then experience only goodness Now.*

Stages Of Migration

Life on earth is a journey that includes many levels and stages. We constantly leave behind much of our physical and cellular past, as well as mental and emotional yesteryears. We are constant migrants, journeying towards origin and the state before creation.

The foetus migrates from the cosy womb to the outside world to face many changes culminating in the final major migration of death, where our material side returns to earth and our spirit re-joins its field of spirits. Everything changes and transforms except the soul, which provides life and consciousness as a divine agent.

> *Human migration is from material concerns to energies and light. Our journey on earth is towards boundlessness and spirithood.*

10. GUIDANCE

Inner & Outer Change

Some people hope to impact upon the world or leave it better than when found. From childhood we always expect to have better times ahead and to experience better possibilities and understanding. That implies inner changes within body, mind and heart, balanced by outer changes.

With reflection, one realises that the inner and outer states are in constant resonance or entanglement. Personal consciousness, which functions within space and time, nourishes the illusion of being separate from cosmic oneness. When this truth is realised then the concern to perfect the world turns towards the self and its spiritual state. When our inner state is optimum, then the outer world would be easily understood.

> *The self is ever restless and is challenged by inner and outer forces. The light of the soul connects all.*

Resistance To Change

The earth is like a hospital where the self evolves and learns to yield to the heart and soul. Early darkness and confusions can be incentives to awakening and illumination. The majority of human beings are like sleepwalkers at the edge of a sloping high roof—about to fall to destruction and death. This pitiful state is due to habits and resistance to change. Keeping old habits gives the illusion of continuity!

The self fears loss of its illusory identity and thus gives way to stubbornness!

A sleepwalker wants to continue sleepwalking. Any change is resisted by the mind – unless it reinforces past habits.

10. GUIDANCE

Breaking Habits

A pleasurable activity is reinforced when shared with others who reinforce the same feeling. The human animal is habit-forming and that is at the root of cultures and civilisations. The mind looks for affirmation and every experience leaves its traces. The more often those experiences are activated, the deeper and more real the memory becomes. Individual and group personalities come about in cycles and follow special archetypal patterns.

Repetition simulates continuity and eternity, which is the condition of our soul. To tap into higher consciousness and the soul's energy fields we need to leave our human limitations by transcending mind and identity. Deliberate breaking of personal habits is a good step towards spiritual evolvement.

> *The self connects the body, mind and soul. Habits enforce identity and breaking them is a step towards Reality.*

In Tune

The task of maintaining a healthy body and mind is relentless. So is the need to tune to heart and listen to it. There we may hear our perfect soul.

With regular meditation and reflection, we regularly experience the delightful light of the soul. Our quest for health and contentment is a prelude to unison with our soul, which transmits these qualities.

We need a sound mind and a pure heart. We cannot deny our earthliness, but need to refer constantly to our heavenliness. Then we may experience wholesomeness.

To be in balance at physical, mental, and spiritual levels of beingness, we need to listen and respond with healing affection.

10. GUIDANCE

Heart To Heart

Adult relationships contain higher aspects of intellect, creativity, spirituality or religion. Initial connectedness at the physical and mental levels; move on towards subtler heart and soul zones. Communication affects the body and limbs, whereas the heart connection is super charged and its effect is deeper in the positive sense, as well as the negative. Heart to heart implies a deep effect. The mind functions at the realm of change and duality, whereas the heart relates to the soul with higher potency and effect.

Our journey is towards perfection and that is the realm of the soul and heart. Love is the unifying agent of pluralities and differences and it belongs to the heart and soul.

> *The drive to experience unity and continuity needs the vehicle of the heart. Love is a beam of the soul that penetrates a pure heart.*

SPECTRUM OF REALITY

Enter Through The Door

For every entity or system, there is a key to connect with it, interact and exit. For success in life, we must know how to relate and connect appropriately and effectively, otherwise frustration and confusion will arise.

Every situation has an entry code and protocol which, if ignored, the outcome may be failure. The energy field of guidance implies learning how to enter into a new dynamic field and achieve what was hoped for. Guidance in the world of pluralities morphs into spiritual insights in the realm of higher consciousness—two different levels of guidance.

The house may have many doors and windows, but for efficient viewing enter through the designated door.

10. GUIDANCE

Suffering & New Openings

Most of our evaluations are relative and changeable. Survival needs and cultures dictate much of our values and preferences. Our experiences are based on cycles and changes. Pain and pleasure are a constant cycle. What caused us stress in the past may be the start of ease now.

Suffering is the experience of an undesirable situation. The less emotional involvement we have in an activity, the easier it is to read and understand the event properly. The key is correct assessment. We prefer comfort and ease to afflictions. However, the darkest part of the night is nearer to the start of the day. New openings and opportunities often follow harsh dawns and closures especially along a spiritual path.

> *If you have done all that you can in a situation, then stop, accept, and reflect upon possible opportunities as a result of the dead end.*

Guarding New Openings

Spiritual seekers often keep company with like-minded and like-hearted people. In many old villages and towns most districts were inhabited by a special profession or trade. In modern times with mobility, and transcultural connectedness, we are prone to discuss and express spiritual openings and epiphanies casually. These disclosures can hamper natural spiritual growth. They can bring about jealousies, envies, and even enmity. It is vital to guard early insights to incubate and fill up the heart's spiritual lake, until it overflows naturally. The seeker's enthusiasm needs to be guarded.

> *The ego blocks the soul's light and to express a spiritual state before it is established may delay further progress.*

10. GUIDANCE

Divine Attributes

We love life, power, and the ability to know, hear, see, express and connect. These are key attributes of the soul and Reality. The energy field of any one of these qualities connects with others. This is the beginning of the vastness of the primal designs and forces that govern the visible universe. All these fields emanate from Oneness. The idea of 'original sin' could be a metaphor for experiencing separation and independence from Oneness.

These fields emanate from the soul. Thus, meditation and worship can be understood and experienced when lived. These virtues can heal and help to transcend the mind through higher attributes, to the endless horizon of Oneness.

> *Human consciousness contains the fields of higher values as well as lower egotistic fields. By embracing a divine attribute, we are climbing out of humanity to divinity.*

Fear Of Provision Or Creation

The self is always needy and desires to connect and continue. To transcend conditioned consciousness and the human limitation we must break through the barrier of fear for survival.

To move onto higher consciousness we need to lose the animal self's concerns, transcend norms and dependence on others, and transcend the fear for provision.

The Divine Reality permeates the universe and governs all that there is within human consciousness. To experience Reality we need to go past all fears and concerns that relate to our humanity and touch the perfection of the One Reality – cosmic divinity.

Fear of provision and desire for acknowledgement by others are natural barriers to Higher Reality.

10. GUIDANCE

Sorrows, Fears & Expectations

Sorrow is due to what has been missed or what is not attainable. We expect and hope for increase and resent reduction. The arc of consciousness leads upwards.

Fear is an important emotion and it helps us not to repeat mistakes and to avoid misery, despondency or despair.

Fear and sorrow are natural afflictions which can be overcome by transcending the mind. Another cause of suffering is the expectation and hope for pleasures, which are naturally accompanied by pain. The ego self always seeks expansion and ease, and as such, will cause disappointments, regrets and blames.

The soul has neither fear nor sorrow; the mind is the seat of these emotions, which can be helpful for survival but handicaps for arrival.

SPECTRUM OF REALITY

Who Is Your Teacher?

The mother helps the toddler to stand and walk. Nurture helps nature. Then come training, instruction and grooming, lessons and teachers, mistakes, knowledge, discipline success and failure. With wisdom, reflection and insight you may hear the inner teacher, your own soul.

Whilst the body and mind are evolving we need teachers and mentors with clear minds, strong intellects and rational skills. For spiritual growth, we need a teacher who has access to higher consciousness and is illumined by personal experience of inner light. We may need different teachers all of whom emerged because of the One. What matters most is the journey from self to soul.

> *We are impressionable creatures and need outer references until we can access our own inner soul—the resident teacher.*

10. GUIDANCE

Following Instructions

Children follow their whims and parents complain about their behaviour. The young mind is excited with curiosity and inquisitiveness. With maturity, it acquires discipline and focus.

Success of any endeavour follows clear intention, attention and appropriate action at the right time and place. Our ancestors looked up to shamans, prophets and teachers of wisdom and enlightenment. Empathy and connection with a teacher increase with love and respect. For wisdom, the teaching context is vital. What is relevant for one person may be inappropriate for another. The successful seeker follows head and heart along the right direction.

We want guidance that shows us the truth within our own heart. We need commitment and consistency along the path so the self yields to its root and origin – the inner soul.

Steps To Awakening

Our life's journey is steps towards a better understanding of our human cosmology and Reality.

The spiritual seeker may experience three steps towards transcendent experience. The first step is to override mind, memory, identity. The second step is entry into deep meditation beyond mind and senses. Then comes the range of experiences of higher consciousness with its beauty, majesty, lights, insights and epiphanies. What remains is to maintain the state of balanced well-beingness of one's humanity and divinity.

> *Kilograms of physical skin are shed every year. To be with the inner soul we need to shed our mental habits and memories, and then we may be close to illumination.*

10. GUIDANCE

Mindfulness & Mindlessness

A healthy mind is a medium that connects energy and matter with meanings and value. A fresh mind evaluates new events and experiences and considers advantages and benefits for fulfilment. Nowadays, the idea of mindfulness implies being focused and single pointed. Mindlessness may equate to oblivion without any sense of time or identity.

The beginner's mind is less cluttered with memories and prejudices. It connects the ever-changing consciousness, with supreme consciousness. It has a chance to transcend personal discernment and evaluation to higher states of pure witnessing.

The beginner's mind is fresh, flexible, and close to the door of eternal presence and the infinite Nowness.

Judge, Repent & Witness

It is in human nature to reach quick conclusions and take appropriate action. With wisdom we reflect and consider wider factors in the situation before we judge. A clear mind with higher intellect could evaluate the situation with the insight and the light of the heart.

The mature and wise mind leads towards spiritual wisdom and understanding. The spiritually awakened witnesses the outer and the inner aspects of the event, and then acts with reference to higher consciousness and durable goodness. Selflessness, compassion and magnanimity lead to clear witnessing and illumination of heart.

> *The awakened person looks at situations and events through higher consciousness. Clear witnessing ends regrets and confusions.*

10. GUIDANCE

Self-Punishment

Most religions place God beyond punishing or vengeful being and describe afflictions as self-inflicted. It is through the mystery of life that we are conscious of consciousness.

When we act due to fear of survival, confusion in mind and emotional reactions may lead to regret, guilt and self-punishment. If one lives fully in the present moment aware of intention and action, then one may avoid harmful action and its repercussions. Presence of mind and heart is needed. Self hurt experiences regret or blame.

The real you is ever present as your soul and to realise that and live it you need to transcend all and enter the zone of the soul's presence.

Serving Others As Yourself

Spiritual growth is enhanced by attention to and understanding of all of creation. When human consciousness evolved and the idea of God consciousness and religious practices spread, service to others for 'God's-sake' became an important prescription. We admire altruism, heroism, magnanimity and greatness of spirit.

The enlightened being only acts by unconditional love and pure consciousness, without expectations of discernible rewards. This service liberates the seeker from the darkness of the ego and the illusion of separation from the One. Your soul serves you unconditionally. Now try to serve others.

To serve unconditionally is to liberate yourself from the calculating mind and ego.

10. GUIDANCE

Appropriateness & Context

An appropriate action or inaction is efficient connectedness along the natural course of time and events. Appropriate eating is when it is done with the right attitude and according to one's own capacity and needs. It is balance, harmony and contentment in life that is the constant objective. It is from the state of neutrality that we experience flashes of higher soul consciousness.

Knowledge of appropriateness is a life skill that can be learnt from educators and books until one takes to it, but it really asks for educators and masters who are experts at it. Ultimately, appropriateness implies presence of mind and heart so that there will be no regrets or guilt. It will be flowing with destiny.

Appropriateness implies clear intention, appropriate action and full presence in the moment—preludes for spiritual awakening.

Morality

Human values and religious teachings attempt to bring about inner stability and communal bonding based on peace, justice and cooperation. Education and grooming increases one's level of consciousness. Good upbringing implies adhering to codes of conduct to maintain harmony and goodness for all.

The higher the consciousness we pursue, the more likely we are to experience wholesomeness and contentment. Our responsibility and respect for other beings stems from divine consciousness, which is ever-present and supreme.

> *The highest level of morality is to respond to the voice of truth, as it emanates from the pure heart.*

10. GUIDANCE

To Mimic & Admire

We cover our ignorance about our true nature with the roles that we play in life. Backed up by memory, we develop an identity. Moreover, we try to emulate others whom we consider are more successful or better role models in order to become more powerful, more loved, efficient or successful.

We are naturally attracted to those considered better. The soul's perfection drives the self towards its own perfection. That is spiritual excellence.

Mimicking others is more likely to detract from evolving to their state. Learning and emulating may change your mental state and conduct, whereas mere mimicking is unlikely to bring about sustainable behavioural change.

To mimic the stroke of a golf champion can be helpful, but to mimic a sage may be a dangerous distraction. Love, follow, and be transformed.

Love As A Climbing Rope

The desire to love and be loved is a natural force to connect and experience some unity and oneness. Human love is the first step towards love of the soul. Your beloved carries a soul, which is the same as yours – your real soul mate!

Love brings with it a passionate dedication and attention that may exclude other emotions. Love of this world is a small aspect of love for truth and the original source and cause of life. Without transcending the physical and discernible, to its meaning and origin, one remains trapped within the box of space-time limitations. Divine love connects and unifies the seen and the unseen and its light permeates all facets of love. Love emanates and returns to the One.

> *Like knowledge, love is a force that leads to the original source of existence—Oneness.*

10. GUIDANCE

Present Presence

The past is not present. Neither is the future. Now is present and is the connection with timelessness and all times. The present connects with its original timelessness.

The present carries traces of all times and singularity before the birth of the universe. Now is constant and yet leaves its traces in the past, pointing towards the future.

The mind's nature is agitation and its present moment is moving. When transcending the mind, one enters Now's presence. That timelessness is the doorway to infinite delights.

> *The future is being shaped in the present and the past had its presence. Now is fully present.*

Relief From Envy & Jealousy

Envy, jealousy and other disturbing emotions are caused by expectations, ambitions and comparison with others' situations. The mind experiences sadness, pain, discontentment and other unpleasant feelings. Intellect and higher consciousness may reveal the root of envy and jealousy or sadness or unhappiness.

Only by access to higher consciousness do we realise the trap of mind, senses and memory. Relief is experienced by transcending thoughts and identity. Then the soul is unburdened.

Experience of the greater lights of heart and soul can bring relief from mental attachments, desires and false hopes. Human suffering can be a prelude to the gift of spiritual offerings.

10. GUIDANCE

A Remedy Or Poison

There is no pleasure without pain. In seeking peace and harmony, you may exert force and aggression. What may appeal to your evolving ego may be an affliction upon your heart. Sensory pleasure and indulgence may cause harm to your body as well as to mind and heart.

What may enhance your earthly consciousness and give you material security may be detrimental for your higher consciousness and spiritual progress. Earthly difficulties may lead to spiritual ease.

A remedy may be bitter and a poison may be sweet. What may please your ego can darken the heart.

Ego As Foe & Old Friend

Humans have two zones of life. One is a living, growing, evolving self, centred in the mind and body. The other is an ever-constant, mysterious soul and source of life. The confusion of personal duality is part of natural growth and evolvement. The ego and personal identity is a natural cover for the sacred soul. Our journey is from the gross to the subtle, from matter to light.

We condemn the ego or self and blame it for our darkness and ignorance. With spiritual wisdom, we discern its original usefulness. The illusion of duality is a driving force in life towards unity. The awakened person was a self and now is a soul. Perfect destiny.

The ego is a natural protector of the soul early in life. Its usefulness becomes obvious as a shell over a delicate pearl.

10. GUIDANCE

Condemn The Action Not The Person

Human consciousness leads to judgements. Do I go this way or that way? What is better for the future? We make decisions based on our quest for balance, well-beingness and happiness. Sometimes our intentions and actions may clash with others and cause discord, animosities, and other times they bring friendship.

If we are on a course of action and someone causes an impediment or obstruction, we try to overcome the obstacle and even condemn the person who caused the difficulty. The mind tries to pigeonhole entities as good or bad, but the same person that caused bad may cause, in another sense, much good.

We live in a world of duality with one aspect stronger than the other, which requires discernment. The worst poison is sometimes a remedy. Use head and heart to gain wisdom and good outcome.

Sublimate Major Problems

Most of our physical and mental challenges need experience, skills and hopeful engagement. Sometimes, a challenge can be overwhelming. No solution appears to a mind or heart that has been exposed to prolonged stress, frustration and depression.

This undesirable situation can be an opportunity to address higher consciousness for appropriate guidance. Problem solvers remain hovering at conditioned consciousness and its limitations. We need to get out of the box and look at a new and wider horizon in order to experience lights and insights.

When our sensory world and mind cannot tackle or resolve an issue, leave it, and sublimate. Beyond the elusive solution lies a new resolution.

10. GUIDANCE

Moderately Extreme

Human life is in balance between two extremes; birth and death, sleep and wakefulness, and wellness and illness and other dualities. Stability, peace and well-beingness require moderation. To awaken to higher consciousness we need to go to the edge of normal consciousness and then take a leap of transcendence. Unique experiences require courage and the ability to face the unusual or extreme state.

Body and mind develop slowly and need moderation and continuity. Spiritual openings and insight by their nature are different from normal consciousness and can be extreme. To live as a soul is not common to all and as such is extreme – only few experience that zone.

The mind requires balance, equanimity and sobriety. The heart deals with spiritual lights and delights beyond limitations.

SPECTRUM OF REALITY

Watch For Excess & Waste

The mind is the intermediate reality between temporary, personal identity and the perpetual soul. During the earthly journey we are often infused by the qualities of the soul, such as knowledge, connectedness, love etc.

During our evolvement, we make many mistakes and cause waste. We collect and accumulate much more than what is needed to live well during our earthly journey. Our emotions cause a lot of blame and make a lot of claims, wasting energy and time. Success is to transcend the limiting consciousness of body and mind.

Our earthly journey is temporary and futile, unless it leads to the unison between head and heart. That state leads to soul consciousness.

10. GUIDANCE

To Be At One Follow An Enlightened One

You need a trustworthy friend to help you out of the illusions and confinement of the lower self and identity.

A teacher may show you maps of reality but you have to learn to drive along these routes back to the original beginning, and how your teacher, your friend, companion or partner may reduce your earthly needs and desires, which will soon be replaced by other desires. Try to find someone who knows and experiences truth. Follow that one so that you end up recognising your own soul at the gateway of the one and only One. Thank the teacher as well as others who lead you and mislead you. Thank the One source of all.

The purpose of human life is to experience existence through the lens of Oneness without denying the temporary experience of pluralities.

Reliance On The One

The original light of the One permeates and governs the universe. The quest to know and experience this reality is the fulfilment of human life.

We seek authority and knowledge and try to avoid ignorance and confusion. The self is rebellious and treacherous as it asserts itself. The soul is ever perfect, in unison with The One.

The awakened being experiences Reality and is in constant reference and deference to it. The human quest is the personal realisation of the origin of life and the One source that permeates all that is known and unseen. To go beyond mind, reason and habits to this perfect Presence is the ultimate intelligent act. To know and rely upon real authority is liberation.

The mind and intellect explores the limits of experience. We want the limitless zone of oneness upon which everything depends.

11. It Is

SPECTRUM OF IT IS

- ✠ To Find Soul, Lose Self
- ✠ Who Is The Master Of Your Destiny?
- ✠ Journey By Light
- ✠ The Perfect Moment
- ✠ Sacred Spot
- ✠ Nothing Is Enough
- ✠ It Is All There!
- ✠ Thrill Of Life
- ✠ Personalized God
- ✠ Whom Does God Love?
- ✠ Will Of God
- ✠ Heavenly Attributes
- ✠ Paradise & Hellfire
- ✠ Success, Failure & Victory
- ✠ From Dead To Living
- ✠ Similar & Incomparable
- ✠ Fairness Due To Oneness
- ✠ Gift Of Disasters
- ✠ Effulgence Of Evidence

SPECTRUM OF REALITY

- ✠ Foresight From Insight
- ✠ Dispersed Gatheredness
- ✠ What Changes & What Is Constant
- ✠ Symmetry & Balance
- ✠ Soulmate
- ✠ Quest For The End
- ✠ Full Cup

Introduction

Consciousness and life are mysteries that constantly call attention and reflection in the hope of being understood. They reveal a lot to us and yet much more remains unknowable. Our physical life began as a tiny clot in the womb and as soon as we are conscious of life we start to question why, when, how, who and other meanings and purpose.

The original cosmic light which emerges from singularity is the source from which everything else had emerged. That is the root of all that energises all that exists and appears as pluralities in our minds and experiences –the original Oneness. The ultimate mystery of Reality is that it contains everything known and unknown and it permeates the entire universe. It is the cause of the particle as well as the wave function. It is the source of life, consciousness, time and space.

What we seek is constant and ever alive although our life as humans is juxtaposed between birth and death. Our human soul is the direct source of life and carries the imprint of the unique perpetual Oneness. The human soul replicates the cosmic soul, or God, and is inseparable from it.

We experience life in duality, in the zone of conditioned consciousness. Our origin and destiny is the ever-pervasive unity and our experience of plurality brings with it a drive toward singularity—that is how It Is. The light of the soul trapped in the box of space-time for a while as it returns to its boundless origin. That is what It Is. That is as It Is. Declaring itself. It Is.

To Find Soul, Lose Self

Basic self-hood and identity develops from birth and matures within a few decades. Most of our worldly activities and roles emanate from our habitual familiarity with identity and memory. For worldly success, the general requirements include a healthy and able body, a clear and focused mind, and strong determination, courage and hope. This is the domain of selfhood.

To access the soul within the heart, we need to transcend the limitations of matter and mind. That requires abandonment of previous mental values, identity and culture. To move from conditioned consciousness to soul consciousness, we need transcendence. . This technology is based on meditation and related spiritual practices and ways of life.

To experience the boundless eternal zone of consciousness— the soul's essence— we need to transcend all our human states.

II. IT IS

Who Is The Master Of Your Destiny?

We live in hope and with expectations of good outcomes. We may curb ambitions and desires in expectation of a better destiny. We pray that tomorrow is better than today.

Disappointment, regret and sorrow are due to an imbalance between our state of body, mind and heart, and the outer world. Our intentions and actions may have been inappropriate and out of context. The outcome is determined as interactions between intention, action and the outer world When we understand the inner, and can read the outer correctly, we are in balance and more present in the moment.

A perfect destiny occurs when there is least possible ego—darkness and the grace and light of spiritual intelligence, illumines our journey.

> *The end is where the beginning was: ever constant and present. Supreme consciousness, or God, is the master designer and governor of all.*

Journey By Light

The human soul or spirit is not earthly and needs mind and intellect to deal with earthly pluralities and limitations. That is how the soul relates to earthly darkness whilst remaining a celestial light. The sun's rays and light promote life on earth after its intensity has been reduced considerably.

The mind is the soul's agent to understand and connect earthly realities, changes and causalities. The mind does not contaminate the pure soul. The essence of every human being is a soul. When the soul leaves the earthly realm and the mind ends, all judgement, contradictions and uncertainties vanish. The divine and eternal nature of the soul returns to its contentment—paradise.

> *The soul carries the imprint of cosmic Reality Self/soul interplay reveals the emergence of duality from unity.*

II. IT IS

The Perfect Moment

The drive of consciousness is towards wider and deeper states. Our quest for excellence and perfection is relentless. Our normal consciousness functions in the mode of dualities and pluralities, and that is our life's challenge and our path of evolvement.

The mind pursues reason and rationality, cause and effects, correlations and other connections. Completions and conclusions imply the end of an event or cycle. In that moment of success or achievement there is stillness, peace and perfection. In this state of peace or inaction lies the secret of the perfect moment of timelessness.

Our origin and essence is perpetual in its perfect beingness and that state is what we aspire for in all our endeavours.

We occasionally experience the perfect moment— no thought, intention or action. That instant reveals our soul's perfect state.

Sacred Spot

There have been endless feuds and warfare regarding what is considered as sacred, sacrosanct and revered. Due to historical accidents and events, a geographic spot takes on the position as a holy place. Popular attitudes, habits, traditions, the passage of time and subtler forces and energies bestow sanctity upon a cave, shrine, river or a mountain. Naturally visitors experience special feelings and imagine divine inspirations. Pilgrimage is often to be at a certain place and certain time where we hope to experience special energy or divine power.

The entire universe had emerged from no-thingness and any place or time can be a symbol that indicates cosmic sacredness and divine presence. As such the whole universe is sacred.

Human identity forever seeks sacred reality within the creational limitations of space and time. Sacred places are reminders of the nature of our own soul.

II. IT IS

Nothing Is Enough

We are naturally inquisitive and acquisitive. Possessions, increase material security, status and other feel-good emotions. Yet nothing is enough. All material pursuits come with greed and troubles. Why do we do it?

Whatever there is in the universe expands and so does our mind and horizons. With insights, spiritual openings and transcendence of the physical world, our natural greed takes on a higher direction towards boundlessness and the eternal—the nature of our soul. As the soul has no needs, therefore nothing is ever enough for the self as it shadows the soul.

It is only through the light of our soul that we are content beyond qualities and quantities, otherwise nothing is ever enough.

It Is All There!

The greatest mystery of life is the seamless connection between limited consciousness and total consciousness. Humanity is derived from divinity. That implies inseparability from the original Oneness.

We love life and are apprehensive about death; yet we have the potential of experiencing the perpetuity of life. It is only personal life that is caught within space and time, whereas Life in partnership with Consciousness is eternal. Numerous energy fields as well as chemical, physical and other lights weave together our physicality. The human soul reflects everything in the universe, at any time. We are journeying towards a destiny that was at the origin and the knowledge of this truth is encrypted within our souls. It has always been there.

Our quest to know and understand Reality stems from our souls. The pattern and plan is well in place and our role is simply to follow the design. Enjoy Grace.

II. IT IS

Thrill Of Life

Every instant is different—new, an endless movement of time. Human consciousness changes all the time. We know it changes because our soul consciousness is constant.

Our conditioned consciousness experiences pleasures and pains, friendship and enmity, and happiness and misery. Insights and revelations of higher consciousness illuminate confusions of conflicting dualities and lead to flashes of the thrill of unity. That thrill takes us away from continuous mental challenges and leads us to what is often described as bliss and paradise. That same state of perfection is embedded in the here and now. Life can be a journey of thrills.

The human desire for miracles is a thread in the tapestry of life. The ultimate thrill is to know and experience that state of infinitude. That is the quantum shift and thrill.

Personalized God

The story of the fall of Adam implies the rise of mind and separate consciousness. The quest for higher consciousness means the conscious effort needed by Adam's offspring to return to origin. Separation and the experience of personal identity and the drive for survival are material foundations in the quest for spiritual awakening and total consciousness.

To seek the ultimate in power, wealth and other divine attributes and qualities, we need to transcend thoughts and memory and rely upon the energy fields that radiate from the original sacred light—personalized as the soul within.

> *Human life is due to the light that is emitted from the sacred soul within the heart. That is the Lord within.*

II. IT IS

Whom Does God Love?

It is an illusion to expect continuous contentment and happiness. There is always a need for something else. For the few who are able to transcend human identity to higher consciousness – there is the experience of joy.

The religious self seeks constant reassurance of divine love and grace, which is provided by the spirit or soul within the heart. This love is irrevocable, constant, and unconditional.

Body, mind, emotions and heart are all nourished from the soul. That is God's love. This love is upheld by human gratitude, acknowledgement, dedicated worship and experience of the divine presence.

> *Divine love is the cosmic energy field that permeates the whole universe and manifests as the human soul within the heart— proof of God's love.*

Will Of God

An important human drive is to express willpower. Much of the time our desires are not fulfilled. Other times we experience regret or sorrow. Desire and personal will are unreliable drives for fulfilment and often cause regrets or grief. The desire to foresee outcomes in our earthly experience and relationships is dominant in our life.

Your will is a small part of your destiny. You have a choice in what you will and act upon but cannot control your destiny. That is God's will, which also includes your will and countless other wills and forces, seen, and unseen. That is fate. The intelligent being reflects and meditates upon God's will to make his own will part of that. That is enlightenment in action.

> *We desire a life that increases in its knowledge, contentment and happiness and that state relates to the soul's nature—God's will.*

II. IT IS

Heavenly Attributes

Humans evolved to regard certain qualities of conduct and morality as desirable and necessary for the future. Several world religions regard Adam as a steward on earth embodying godly attributes. The metaphor of Adam refers to the human spirit or soul.

Human souls carry the imprint of desirable attributes which are reflected through the minds of humans. Spiritual progress is living these attributes, which lead to higher consciousness, universal connectedness and ongoingness. Higher qualities can be thought of as spiritual ladders and ropes that enable the human animal to live as a spiritual being, in transition towards the original state.

To live as a soul, the animal self needs to be held within bounds; and then to transcend sensory experiences to the abode of perfect Grace.

Paradise & Hellfire

The human drive points towards wider and deeper consciousness and experience of lasting contentment and happiness. With some wisdom, we realize that all positive feelings and experiences are accompanied by negative ones. There is no gain without a loss or good without a bad.

Our earthly experiences are limited and conditioned by what is considered as attractive or repulsive. Obstacles and challenges surround our mental image of paradise. Paradise of the hereafter is beyond time and space and religious hell represents a state of total confusion and breakdown. It takes grace and fortune to slip out of darkness into light, from mind to soul from terrestrial to celestial.

> *Our consciousness is in two zones; one is the earthly limited zone and is never secure. The other is total consciousness of light and delight.*

II. IT IS

Success, Failure & Victory

Constant success is what we really desire: enviable steps that lead to perfect destiny.

Contentment is what we long for. Failure is disconnection and discontinuation. The self resents this state, which is the opposite of the soul's normal state.

Lasting success or continuous victory can be imagined when you turn away from all worldly pursuits and needs. Lasting success implies constant access to absolute Reality as experienced by the soul within the heart. It is the domain where all dualities end and the sacred light prevails. It is the zone where there is only joy.

Failure and success are the dualities that challenge our humanity. Victory belongs to our soul and the world of spirits.

From Dead To Living

Creation began from nothing discernible and after a period, consciousness and life began on earth. From dead matter life arose in a single cell, brought about by the alchemy of water, air, heat and light. A few hundred million years later this basic life evolved to become human beings.

The mind is the software that dwells within the brain hardware. The mystery of consciousness triggers life into independent and self-aware entities as we are.

The cycles of life and death are inseparable as one leads to the other. Living plants are nourished through decomposed materials. Without death, there will be no rejuvenation and upward movement in consciousness.

A fresh thought arises from a still mind. Both visibly and invisibly, life arises from what we call dead or inert.

II. IT IS

Similar & Incomparable

Sameness and otherness overflow from Oneness—the incomparable One, unique and all pervasive, the Cause of the universe.

Body and mind are time-dependant whereas our soul is not subject to time or place. All human beings are similar in this basic composition. We are driven by the desire to connect and relate and to experience continuity and eternity—that is the nature of the One incomparable originator, the source of power and life. That incomparable truth is within the human soul and the purpose of life is to discover, know and experience this unique Reality.

> *In our outer appearance we all seem different, yet in our quest and desire we are the same. Reality or God is sublime, incomparable Light of lights. That uniqueness is reflected in our own soul.*

Fairness Due To Oneness

Desire for fairness and justice is a great unifying factor for humans. Much enmity, opposition and discord is due to what has been perceived as unfair or unjust. The implication is that the basic human template is common to all. We desire durable and pleasant connections and interactions. We aspire for contentment and a life of leisure and contemplation.

We generally prefer harmony, friendship and acceptance to discord and rejection. Connectedness is a manifestation of Oneness. Our search for an original cause is part of the truth of universal Oneness. That is the drive for human fairness and equality.

Our desire for truth, justice and fairness is a beam of light that emanates from Oneness and pervades the universe — from where all has emanated.

II. IT IS

Gift Of Disasters

We love comfort and ease. The wise reflect upon difficulty with anticipation of deeper understanding and insights. It is the mind's conditioned consciousness that judges events as good or bad. Survival, concern and consciousness veil perfections. The awakened being regards the calamity as a prelude to renewal and new possibilities for deeper illumination. In pure consciousness there are no difficulties. The light of the soul is beyond ease or difficulty.

With intense afflictions, the mind gives up. Then the soul's light may be perceived. When humanity gives up, divinity may become clear.

When a setback is seen through the lens of the soul, it can be perceived as an opportunity to return to the ascent towards the Truth.

Effulgence Of Evidence

Everything in existence reveals aspects of its dominant nature, limitations and reality. Nothing is concealed from higher consciousness. Every atom transmits its frequency and every creature pursues its need for survival and continuity. The evidence is there if we can hear, feel or read it by heart or mind.

Whatever we pursue in life is toward a state of balance, peace and harmony between body, mind and heart. Every intention, attention and action reveals a need to be fulfilled. Everything is heading toward completion. Success and contentment relate to the durability of well-beingness, peace and contentment at soul.

Every movement and action declares its purpose. Ultimately, spiritual stillness implies access to higher consciousness that is beyond drives and needs.

II. IT IS

Foresight From Insight

We are explorers in space and time. We ask: who are we? Where are we and where are we going to? We are obsessed about the future. Hope is the expectation that tomorrow may be better than today. We all want a better future for coming generations.

We seek the company of wise people who have greater knowledge and can answer the numerous 'why' questions in the hope that we may be liberated from suffering. The future is a natural continuation of the present moment. A sage may give us glimpses of what is to come and other people may be helpful to avert disasters. Wisdom and insights are necessary backgrounds to be on the path that leads to a desirable destiny. The more insight we have the greater will be our foresight.

A human being is a product of the past and the present. The future is a continuation of that stream of consciousness modified by will and interactions.

SPECTRUM OF REALITY

Dispersed Gatheredness

The surface of the vast ocean hides an aquatic universe underneath it. Our thin veneer of humanity veils the immensity of our soul's universe. Due to cultural mores of politeness, people may appear as friendly, cooperative and loving, whereas just beneath the surface simmers a volcano of animosities, conflicting interests and discord, all about to erupt.

In many gatherings, you notice people being outwardly friendly toward each other, smile politely and act as civilized beings. In reality, at the mental level, there may be little connectedness or real empathy. As for the heart, there is no love. This is the nature of most gatherings of dispersed hearts. When the mind is dominant and the heart is dormant.

Outward togetherness does not imply inner gatheredness. What appears on the surface as pleasant conduct may hide deep discord and repulsion.

II. IT IS

What Changes & What Is Constant

Life evolves due to countless interactions and changes in desires and directions. We are moved by love for survival, desires, challenges, hopes, as well as despairs. We are caught within countless forces that constantly change and interact.

Psychic phenomena, religious inspiration, spiritual pursuits and other ideas may attract our attention. All of these often lead to terrains that are difficult or dangerous to traverse. All thoughts occur within the existential domain and as such are veils of Reality. Only when thoughts stop and identity is lost can one be at the door of sacred Presence.

Anything that moves and changes is subject to the limitations of space and time and has a temporary reality. The Real is ever constant.

SPECTRUM OF REALITY

Symmetry & Balance

Plurality and duality cascade into existence through numerous levels and layers of discernibility. Our innate intelligence looks for original causes, differentiation between similarities and opposites. Symmetries are often considered beautiful and natural. Each human being is a modified copy of the genetic mix of parents and ancestors. There is much causality, balanced connectedness and a few subtle scripts written therein with invisible ink.

Our life is a complex web of connectedness with numerous beginnings and ends; each form is balanced by a meaning between cause and effect. We are held between our body, mind and soul, matters and energies.

Consciously and subconsciously, we are balanced between life forces interacting within time and space.

II. IT IS

Soulmate

A soulmate is another being who enhances the quality of your life, your spiritual evolvement and well-beingness. Marriage and partnership may be more durable if it is between two soulmates—each reflecting Reality and Truth to the other.

For a young couple attracted to each other the question is to consider love and attraction after the early novelty of a relationship has worn off. Soulmates' love deepens with time.

The physical and mental attraction in relationships is likely to wear off and what is more durable relates to intellect and heart where there is lasting unity in the closeness of souls.

> *Looking for a soulmate is an outer drive energized by your own soul within you—the ever-present soulmate.*

Quest For The End

We experience numerous spheres of cycles and zones of consciousness with natural beginnings and ends. Our breathing, heartbeats, sleeping and waking, and the numerous mental functions, are all cyclical events drifting within space and time.

A natural extension of all these experiences is the desire to know the nature of the ultimate end, and what lies beyond it. The soul carries the memory of cosmic patterns that we experience and we quest after that knowledge. We are driven to discover the original state — the sacred Oneness that is ever there.

> *Sleep puts an end to our wakeful state and transcendence of mind takes us to the doorway of the infinite, eternal Light. One state ends for the other to begin.*

II. IT IS

Full Cup

Your cup is full and you are content and joyful—for a while. Most people suffer from empty cups—there is always a need or a desire. When your cup is full, your universe is complete, for a while.

Your soul's light shines bright when the heart is clear. Then body and soul are in unison—fulfilment is experienced.

The nourishment, solace and thrill that your soul beams at you is utter bliss. Even patience and limitations become sweet—this is when you are accessing timelessness.

> *The fulfilled authentic being experiences splendid presence whilst journeying in a changing world. Your soul has filled you up.*

SPECTRUM OF REALITY
ABOUT THE AUTHOR

Shaykh Fadhlalla Haeri is a spiritual philosopher and writer whose role as a teacher grew naturally out of his own quest for self-fulfillment. Since childhood he has been attracted to scientific investigation and intellectual pursuit. After a stint in industry and consulting, he embarked on teaching, writing and meditating.

His awareness of global realpolitik compelled him to seek a truth that would reconcile the past with the present, the East and West. His discovery affirms that One Cosmic Reality is the source behind all known and unknown states.

Shaykh Haeri's unifying perspective emphasizes practical, actionable knowledge of self-transformation. It provides a natural bridge between different approaches to spirituality, offering common ground of higher knowledge for various religions, sects and secular outlooks. With a lifetime's experience of contemplation, research, and insights, he shares what it means to live in the light of the Absolute in a relative world and maintains that spiritual awakening is potentially available to all.

NOTES

NOTES